THE EMPEROR
AND THE
ELEPHANTS

A PEACE CORPS VOLUNTEER'S STORY OF LIFE DURING
THE LATE 1970S IN THE CENTRAL AFRICAN EMPIRE

RICHARD W. CARROLL

A PEACE CORPS WRITERS BOOK

THE EMPEROR AND THE ELEPHANTS: A PEACE CORPS VOLUNTEER'S STORY OF
LIFE DURING THE LATE 1970S IN THE CENTRAL AFRICAN EMPIRE
A PEACE CORPS WRITERS BOOK
An imprint of Peace Corps Worldwide

Printed in the United States of America
by Peace Corps Writers of Oakland, California.

For more information, contact peacecorpsworldwide@gmail.com.
Peace Corps Writers and the Peace Corps Writers colophon are trademarks of
PeaceCorpsWorldwide.org.

ISBN-13: 9781935925705
ISBN-10: 1935925709

First Peace Corps Writers Edition, 2016

*To my children, Deva Rae, Orion Wallbridge, and Dylan Forest
that they may better know their father who loves them so.*

PREFACE

O n 15 September 1975 at Mt. Katahdan, the northern terminus of the Appalachian Trail, I took the last steps of a five-month hike. Elated with the completion of one of my most profound experiences to date, I placed a collect call home from Baxter State Park. After having rejected an invitation from the Peace Corps to do shrimp farming in the Philippines while I was hiking in the Shenandoahs, another invitation awaited me on the kitchen table of our old farmhouse in Cheshire, Connecticut. My mother opened the letter and read it to me over the phone. I was being asked to go to the Central African Republic (CAR) to serve as a fisheries extension agent. Another white blaze, a waypoint like the trail markers I had followed for many months.

I was due to begin training and leave for Africa in the summer. The next three seasons brought a transition from the Appalachian hills to the heart of Africa, as well as transitions in my family. In addition to the excitement about my Peace Corps invitation, my mother told me of the death of my cousin Bob, who lived next door. Stunned by the news, I thought about the last time I had seen him, just a few months earlier when I had taken my "vacation" from the trail and came home to help with some of the larger tasks of maintaining a large farmhouse in the country. Bob was my mother's favorite of all her nephews. She taught him how to swim and to drive, always kidding and gently prodding him. When he wanted to marry his sweetheart, Doris, my parents gave him two acres on the corner of our 20-acre turkey farm where he built his dream house, married Doris, and had two children, Robby and Cindy.

After getting the bad news from my mother, I made my way to the Maine Turnpike with a hand-lettered sign that said "HELP." It was dark and rainy, with cars speeding and splashing by, a far cry from the path in the woods I just left. A state trooper saw the sign and stopped for me. He was sympathetic to my story and drove me to the Bangor Airport, where I picked up a free flight to Hartford, Connecticut.

The next morning I went to a funeral home in Hamden that was full of family. Bob was a cousin, a neighbor, almost a big brother, almost my mother's son. My mother didn't have her first child until she was well into her forties and up until then thought she would never have children of her own. Before my sister and I were born, Bob was her boy. Bob's children, Robby and Cindy, though a bit younger, were close to my sister Lynn and me. Lynn taught Cindy how to ride horses, and she kept her pony, Sparky, in the converted-turkey-coop horse barn in our back lot. Robby would always fall into or onto something, and I remember carrying him crying back to our house more than once when he stepped on a nail and my mother had to take him to Dr. Armbruster's for a tetanus shot.

At the end of the next month I got a call from my girlfriend Darien's mother, who had the look, personality, and voice of Ursula the sea witch. She worked in the emergency department at Yale-New Haven Hospital, and called to tell me my father had just been brought to the E.R. in an ambulance. My mother, sister, and I drove to New Haven Hospital and found my father lying on a gurney ready to go to the morgue. He had advanced stenosis in his heart valves, but had been afraid of the fairly new surgery to open the arteries, which is routine now.

The winter of change was long, and my grandmother died after suffering a broken hip at 91. Just a few months earlier she had been forced to leave her little house on Bantam Street in North Haven on the Quinnipiac River. It was a beautiful spot when we were kids, full of birds and frogs, but as the highways and bridges kept narrowing the wide river, it would flood its banks and inundate her house. She was at least 90 years old when my father and I had to carry her from her house to higher ground, walking hip deep in the raging brown water swirling down the road. We hauled her in a chair to a rowboat that we pushed to higher ground and then lifted her to our car. When the house was no longer habitable she went into a nursing home, which she hated.

My mother was in the ambulance with her on the way to the hospital when she broke her hip and listened as my grandmother looked outside and picked out the landmarks of her life; the tower on West Rock where a nature center used to be, the Magic Mile shopping center in the place where she picked blackberries as a girl. Her world was swept away by the river.

To me the funerals were signposts indicating a path ahead like the white blazes that mark the Appalachian Trail. I understood for the first time how short life is and how quickly it can change. I felt a surge of desire to live my life deliberately, so I wouldn't, as Thoreau wrote, "discover that when my time came to die that I had not lived." I felt the weight of my parents' thwarted dreams and aspirations that were unfulfilled and led to lives out of balance.

My mother wanted to be a nurse, but she wasn't accepted to nursing school due to a heart murmur. My father wanted to be a physician, but had to leave the University of Connecticut when he ran out of money for food. Unable to pursue careers in medicine, my parents moved from their small, tidy house on Long Island Sound in West Haven and bought a four story, 28-room hunting lodge built in 1910 in Cheshire to go back to the land and become farmers. My father loved sailing, but gave up his boat and borrowed the $5,000 to buy the house and 20 acres. The brook that flowed through the property had been blocked by a cement dam to form a pond, which broke during a hurricane in 1938, leaving twisted trees and upended roots. The handsome young couple, full of life, set to clear the land and become pioneers in the turkey business. They cut the wood with their Farmall Cub tractor and burned the logs in the basement furnace and the two huge, tile-inlaid fireplaces in the living room and dining room. The beams and woodwork throughout the house were chestnut wood and a wood swing hung from the 12" x 12" beams crossing the living room. The third-floor attic was a finished servants' quarters, complete with buzzers to the kitchen below. When the lodge was first built there were moose, bear, and deer in the woods and native brook trout in the stream.

When they bought it in 1944, it was more than a fixer-upper. My mother who prided herself on her svelte figure, tanned skin, and strong swimming, became a farm woman, hauling wood and dressing the beheaded turkeys my father brought into the cold, wet basement. My mother would scald, pluck, and process the birds. We had a huge, cork-lined, walk-in freezer in the basement that would be full, especially around holiday times. My mother's family from the city would show up on weekends, set up chairs, and watch my father plow the fields, while my mother cooked for the crowd. The romance of moving back to the land wore off after the initial profits they saw from the turkey business dropped when the big producers took over most of the poultry supply. Even though my parents had high hatch rates through natural rearing, the price of the feed became more than the price they could charge for their turkeys, and after a few years they could barely make ends meet.

My father then joined the Connecticut State Police, where he created his legacy by helping to develop the alcoholmeter, now known as the breathalyzer used to determine whether someone was driving under the influence. When World War II broke out, he wanted to join the service to try again for a medical degree. The State Police wouldn't let him leave as this was now considered his service to his country. After the war, my father became a foreman at a wire factory, then went into real estate, until he died at the age of 65 in 1975.

It was my father's death and the circumstances that led to it that made me determined to live with my eyes open, to see the signposts along my way, and to live in the now. I could not work my life away to pursue a quiet retirement at 65 only to end up dead without ever fulfilling my dreams. My father once bought a small, graceful wood sloop that we were going to fix up and sail one day. The boat was perched on stanchions in the backyard. Each season, more fall leaves filled the hull, and spring rain rotted the teak decks. Gradually, it became part of the landscape of broken dreams. The saw that cut the wood in their early days on the farm is still perched on the red rock, a reminder of dreams rusted solid, never to be pursued.

With all this heaviness I felt light. I would fully be with every moment of my life, ready always to give and take the most that I could in life, and to make my living by living fully, a right livelihood.

I set about putting the house in order. I needed to get the house as my mother wanted it and in a way that the house could pay for itself. We converted the attic servants' quarters into an apartment and built an outside staircase up three fights to get to it-like a stairway to heaven. I vividly remember carrying full sheets of plywood up three stories on a ladder in the wind building the dormer for a rear entrance to the apartment.

Now the time for the next chapter in my life had come. I looked at the atlas and found the country that I would spend the next 30 years living in and living for. As the name suggests, finding Central Africa on the map was the easy part. Getting there, however, took three months of travel and training, and arriving at an understanding of the country itself took 30 years of hard work and dedication. Today, when I reread my posts from my Peace Corps years to the *Cheshire Herald*, our hometown newspaper, I hear the old Bob Dylan lyrics "I was so much older then, I'm younger than that now" in my head and I smile on my naiveté. That was the 70's, I was 23 years old, Dylan was my man, and the glasses were rosy. By adapting those Peace Corps posts, this book expresses the blind passion of that 23-year-old man tempered by the wisdom, and sometimes the cynicism, of myself as a much older and possibly wiser retired conservationist.

INTRODUCTION

Banana Republic or
Backwater Paradise?

The French and Germans began exploring the part of Africa now known as the Central African Republic in the mid-1800's with the goal of stemming the slave trade established by various sultanates. This was a time of outrage in Europe and the U.S. as abolitionists advocated ending the trade in and enslavement of human beings. Territorial expansionism and profit obviously were other significant motives. The French and Belgians fought each other over the boundaries of their colonies and finally settled on the Ubangi River as the border between King Leopold's Congo Free State and the French colony of the Upper Ubangi. The French established companies such as la Compagnie française du Haut-Congo and around 20 other conglomerates that were granted 30-year monopolies to exploit products from the land. Ivory, duiker skins for wallets and handbags, wood, palm oil, and rubber were the top commodities. While eventually closing the major Arab slave-trading operations, they set up their own forced-labor operations in the forest, harvesting the highly valuable wild rubber. When I launched the Dzanga-Sangha Program in the southern dense forest zone of CAR in the early 1980's, I would find wild rubber trees scarred with slashes to tap the sap, deep in the forest, 40 to 50 miles from any road that may have existed at that time. Quotas were set for each worker, and the repercussions were brutal if they were not met.

The Belgians carried the repercussions for missed quotas to the extreme in King Leopold's Congo Free State. In 1884-85 the Congress of Berlin recognized Leopold II, king of Belgium, as the lawful head of the International Association of the Congo, soon to be known as the Congo Free State. Leopold wanted his small country of Belgium to join in the colonization fever, and chose the Congo as his "colony." Although he never visited his private colony, King Leopold held absolute political, judicial, and legislative power in the Congo. All "unoccupied" land was claimed as property of his Association, both unexplored lands and fields lying fallow. The Congo Free State was less a colony than a company built on terror and forced labor.[1]

Leopold died in 1909, having made a profit from the territory conservatively estimated as equal to more than $1.1 billion in the American dollars of a century later. The population of the region fell from over 20 million people in 1891 to 8.5 million in 1922, only to recover somewhat over the next decade to 10 million in 1924.[2]

To force and "incentivize" people to increase their rubber quotas, the soldiers took to hunting humans. Congo soldiers returned from their manhunt with baskets of human hands—men, women, and children's hands—which they laid at the feet of their white commanders to be carefully checked against the cartridges they expended. Officials of the rubber trusts crucified women and children, and decorated the village huts with the intestines and sexual organs of the slaughtered males.[3]

As people resisted the forced labor, the fighting grew worse, and the troops took to killing their prisoners, in one case thirty of them. By the time the campaign was over, one soldier said "we had undergone six weeks of painful marching and had killed over nine hundred natives, men, women and children." The incentive and the cause of the deaths was the potential of "adding fully twenty tons of rubber to the monthly crop."[4]

The basket of hands became the symbol of the Congo Free State. The collection of hands became an end in itself. Belgium Force Publique soldiers brought them to stations in place of rubber: they even went out to harvest them instead of rubber. They became a sort of currency.[1]

An old friend from the World Wildlife Fund made me a hand-painted poster depicting this horror with these quotes. It hangs on the wall in my study, and it is no wonder that these countries have struggled with leadership when the role models from the Western world were so brutal.

The Italian-born, naturalized Frenchman Pierre Savorgnan de Brazza was appointed as the governor general in 1883, and he appointed the commandants for the five "federated" colonies of French Equatorial Africa. His first encounter with Africa was in 1872, sailing with an anti-slavery mission near Gabon. He explored the Ogooué River in Gabon and eventually reached the Congo River, negotiated trading relationships with chiefs in the region, and established a French settlement on the Congo's Malebo Pools, which was eventually named Brazzaville, and become the capital of the Congo. In 1904 Ubangi-Shari was established as a separate colony apart from the French Congo, with Bangui as the capital. Clashes and brutality marked the "concessions" throughout the colony. In 1910 Brazzaville, Congo, became the seat of French Equatorial Africa, which consisted of Gabon, Middle Congo, Ubangi-Shari, and Chad.

Barthélemy Boganda became the first native of Ubangi-Shari to be ordained as a Catholic priest in the late 1930's, and by 1946, he was elected as Deputy of Ubangi-Shari and member of the Grand Council of French

Equatorial Africa. In the next few years, he established the Movement for the Social Evolution of Black Africa (MESAN). Boganda became mayor of Bangui in 1956 and was elected president of the Grand Council of French Equatorial Africa the year after. On 1 December 1958, the autonomous Central African Republic was proclaimed, and Boganda became the first prime minister. Boganda, with the potential to be a solid leader, died in a plane crash in 1959, and David Dacko was elected prime minister. On 13 August 1960, the CAR was proclaimed independent by France, and David Dacko became the first president.

This series of events set the stage for the most memorable leader of the country, Jean-Bidel Bokassa. Bokassa was a cousin of Dacko, and a nephew of Boganda. He was born in Bobangui, 50 miles south of Bangui, as were Boganda and Dacko. His father was publicly executed by the French when he refused to organize rosters of villagers and re-sisted French rule and forced labor. Bokassa's mother committed suicide shortly after the death of her husband. As an orphan, Bokassa was edu-cated by missionaries and joined the French Colonial Army in 1939 as a private. He served with valor in Indochina and rose through the ranks quickly. On 15 August 1944, he participated in the Allied Forces landing in Provence, France. He was inducted into the Légion d'Honneur, and was decorated with the Croix de Guerre. After 23 years of service and a 20 year absence from Africa, he was posted again in Bangui. After inde-pendence, he left the French Army and was given the task of creating a new military as commander in chief. He became CAR's first colonel on 1 December 1964.

During this same time, Dacko was under pressure from independence groups, the Lumumbists from the south (Congo) and the Sudan People's Liberation Army from the east. His own MESAN Party pressured him to move from under France's thumb. He established diplomatic relations with Mao Zedong's People's Republic of China. Bokassa and the French government were concerned about the influence of Communism. Encouraged by the French, including direct intervention by Charles de Gaulle, and fueled by his own ambitions, Bokassa made his move. In what is known as the Saint-Sylvestre coup d'état, on 31 December 1965, Bokassa forced Dacko to resign and announced on the radio that he had taken over to restore justice to the people.

He quickly formed a new government, invalidated the constitution, and dissolved the National Assembly. He told his countrymen that he would give up power once the threat of Communism had been eliminated, the economy stabilized, and corruption rooted out. He allowed MESAN to continue, but barred all other political organizations. In his first months, he imposed new rules and regulations: men and women between ages 18 and 55 had to provide proof that they had jobs, or else they were fined or imprisoned; begging was banned; tom-tom playing was allowed only during the nights and weekends; a "morality brigade" patrolled the bars and dance halls, and polygamy, dowries and female circumcision were all abolished.

Despite their earlier support, France was becoming reluctant to bolster Bokassa. He met with Georges Pompidou in 1966, and when Bokassa threatened to withdraw from the French monetary zone, President Charles de Gaulle sealed French backing by making a state visit to CAR.

In 1971, Bokassa promoted himself to full general, and on 4 March 1972 declared himself president for life. In 1975, the French president Valéry Giscard d'Estaing declared himself a "friend and family member" of Bokassa. France supplied its former colony's regime with financial and military backing. In exchange, Bokassa frequently took d'Estaing on hunting trips in CAR and supplied France with uranium, which was vital for France's nuclear energy and weapons program in the Cold War.

The "friendly and fraternal" cooperation with France reached its peak with the imperial coronation ceremony of Bokassa I on 4 December 1977. The French Defense Minister sent a battalion to secure the ceremony, loaned 17 aircraft to the new Central African Empire's government, and even assigned French Navy personnel to support the orchestra. The coronation lasted for two days and cost between $20 and $30 million, more than the annual budget of the CAR. French artist Jean-Pierre Dupont organized the ceremony, and Parisian jeweler Claudé Bertrand made his crown, which included diamonds valued at $5 million. White columns were constructed along the path that his gilded carriage pulled by white horses would follow, to the Grand Cathedral which housed his golden, eagle-shaped throne. His son and heir sat beside him in regal wear, and his empress, Catherine, sat on his other flank. The entire city and the rest of the country was in forced celebration, and women marched in the parade wearing clothes made of cloth depicting the Emperor and Empress. Now I lived in the Central African Empire.

In 1976, I entered the Peace Corps in CAR as Bokassa declared the republic a monarchy and had himself crowned Sa Majesté Impériale (His Imperial Majesty) Bokassa Premier. In the formal ceremony on 4 December 1977, Bokassa's full title was Empereur de Centrafrique par la volonte du peuple centrafricain, uni au sein du parti politique national, le MESAN (Emperor of Central Africa, by the will of the people, united under the national political party, MESAN). His lavish coronation ceremony was modeled after his hero, Napoleon I of France. The coronation consumed the annual budget of CAR and all of France's aid money for that year. No foreign leaders honored the event with their presence.

In 1979 French newspapers reported that Bokassa had offered the then French Minister of Finance, Valéry Giscard d'Estaing diamonds in 1973. Bokassa's own memoirs valued them at half a million dollars. This developed into a major political scandal known as the Diamond Affair, which cost Giscard d'Estaing his reelection bid. The Franco-Central African relationship took a downward turn when the French also learned of Bokassa's willingness to become a partner with Muammar al-Gaddafi of Libya.

Bokassa met with Gaddafi in 1976. During our Peace Corps training in the town of Mbaiki, in the prefecture of Lobaye, they both rode through the streets in an armored vehicle waving to the crowd, which included me. Gaddafi promised funds, but he was interested in furthering his dream of a sub-Saharan African United Arab States and demanded that Bokassa change his faith to Islam and take on a Muslim name. In a grand public ceremony, Bokassa changed his name to Salah Eddine Ahmed Bokassa. When the money didn't come through, Bokassa abandoned his new faith, which was incompatible with his plans to be crowned emperor in the Catholic cathedral in Bangui, and dropped the new name.

Although Bokassa claimed that the new empire would be a constitutional monarchy, in practice it remained a military dictatorship as before, and suppression of dissenters remained widespread. Torture was rampant, with allegations that even Bokassa himself occasionally participated in beating and executions.

By January 1979, French support for Bokassa had all but eroded after food riots in Bangui led to a massacre of civilians. The final straw came April 17-19 when a large number of elementary students in Bangui and elsewhere in the country were arrested after they had protested against paying for and wearing the expensive, government-required school uniforms with Bokassa's image on them. The uniforms were made in a factory owned by Bokassa or one of his ex-wives. Around 100 children were killed. Bokassa allegedly participated in the massacre, beating some of the children to death with his ebony and ivory cane.

The worldwide press coverage that followed the deaths of the students opened the way for a successful coup, which saw French troops fall from the sky in Bangui in Operation Barracuda, restoring democracy by reinstalling Bokassa's cousin, David Dacko to power. Bokassa was on a state visit to Libya trying again to get bailout funds when the call was made to the French troops waiting in N'Djamena, Chad. Bokassa fled into exile to Abidjan, Ivory Coast, on 20 September 1979 where he lived for 4 years. He then moved to France, where he was allowed to settle in his Château d'Hadricourt in a suburb of Paris. France gave him political asylum because of French Foreign Legion obligations.

Bokassa had been sentenced to death in absentia in December 1980 for the murder of numerous political rivals. However, he returned from exile in France on 24 October 1986 and was immediately arrested on charges of treason, murder, and cannibalism. His return was followed by a yearlong public trial, broadcast on the national radio that kept the country's citizens glued to the radio. Walking down a village lane, one was never out of earshot of Radio Bangui and the trial of Bokassa.

One of the most highly publicized charges against Bokassa was cannibalism. However, the CAR laws forbidding cannibalism classified any crime of eating human remains as a misdemeanor. Eating people a misdemeanor! Upon seizing power from David Dacko in 1981, President André Kolingba had declared amnesty for all misdemeanors committed during the tenure of his predecessors. Bokassa could not be punished for the crime, even if found guilty, even though witnesses testified to cooking human flesh for him. The prosecution did not examine the rumors that

Bokassa had served the flesh of his victims to French president Giscard d'Estaing. Another urban legend is that Bokassa was hosting a diplomatic dinner at Baringo, his guests being ambassadors and such. At the end of the meal, he rose and asked his guests how they liked the meat. Shortly thereafter, Bokassa was dethroned, and a diplomat was found hanging on a meat hook in the freezer with a rump roast removed. It was a diplomatic dinner after all!

On 29 February 1988, President Kolingba demonstrated his opposition to capital punishment by voiding the death penalty against Bokassa and commuted his sentence to life in prison in solitary confinement, but the following year the sentence was reduced to 20 years. With the return of democracy to CAR in 1993, Kolingba declared general amnesty for all prisoners, and Bokassa was released on 1 August 1993.

Bokassa remained in CAR for the rest of his life. In 1996, as his health declined, he proclaimed himself the 13th Apostle and claimed to have secret meetings with the Pope. Bokassa died of a heart attack on 3 November 1996 in Bangui, at the age of 75. He had 17 wives and 50 to 60 children.

As bad as things were in CAR, Bokassa fit in well with the neighborhood! His horrors were not unique in central Africa. Across the Ubangui River in Zaire (ex-Congo Free State), Mobutu Sese Seko, a distant relative of Bokassa, had himself declared Marshal. Though his Authenticity campaign, he renamed the county Zaire and renamed himself Mobutu Sese Seko Kuku Ngbendu Wa Za Banga ("The all-powerful warrior who, because of his endurance and inflexibility appointed to win, goes from conquest to conquest, leaving fire in his wake.") His classic image was his thick framed glasses, walking stick, and leopard-skin toque. Mobuto's Zaire defined kleptocracy and nepotism. His wealth was estimated at $5 billion. The most memorable thing he did was host the Rumble in the Jungle–the match between Mohammad Ali and Joe Fraser in 1974. I recommend watching the 1996 documentary and seeing Ali and Fraser training in the streets of Kinshasa. When HIV/AIDS began infecting Central Africa and putting yet another stigma on this land, Mobutu blamed the epidemic on Ali, Fraser, and their entourage. However, evidence indicates that HIV mutated from a chimp in southeast Cameroon around 1908, and descended the Sangha River, to the Congo River, then to Léopoldville (now Kinshasa). The skewed social structure established under the Belgian regime allowed HIV to run rampant in the crowded city. Mobutu can't be blamed for this.

Like Bokassa, Mobutu allowed for only a targeted distribution of wealth–buying patronage. He bested Bokassa by commissioning the Concord for weekend jaunts to La Moulin Rouge and shopping trips in Paris directly from his enclave in Gbadolite, in eastern Zaire. Keeping the infrastructure in chaos prevented any opposition or civil society from forming. No one dared speak against Bokassa

Development was not a countrywide priority, and the only paved roads or real schools were in the president's home regions. The 125-kilo-meter road to Mbaiki was the only paved road in the country, as this led to Bokassa's home village of Baringo, where he built his residence. The Agricultural University, which the Peace Corps used for training, was at the end of this road. When Bokassa was in residence, there were at least nine to ten roadblocks–police barriers or checkpoints, manned by camo-clad, bored, slightly drunk, usually large men with big guns. It was running the gauntlet getting from Bangui to Mbaiki.

Being from the forest, Bokassa had great respect for the BaAka, or Pygmy groups, preferably called forest foragers. BaAka were a marginalized people, both feared and loathed, considered wizards or animals. Anyone who could live in that inhospitable forest must be an animal. But they were sought after for their magic and knowledge of medicines from the forest. Another urban legend is that an attempt to murder Bokassa with a hand grenade failed, as it rolled between his legs and never detonated, because he was protected by a BaAka magic amulet. Bokassa would deliver speeches on Radio Bangui stating that BaAka are people and that they should be treated with respect.

Baringo was complete with lion and crocodile pits. The animals were always well fed by Bokassa's potential opponents. His form of justice was rather straightforward. A thief had an ear cut off, forever marked for his crime. Caught again, the other ear would be lopped off. A third strike cost a hand. One accused of lying lost his tongue. There was very little crime during the times of Bokassa.

Bokassa was a colonel in the French Army during the colonial period and kept favor with the French. Despite the strong French presence and military bases in CAR, they, in theory, stayed aloof from affairs of State. Actually, the French Ambassador ran the show mostly, but Bokassa was tolerated as he kept Giscard d'Estang in his good graces with gifts of hundreds of thousands of dollars' worth of diamonds. He was protective of Giscard's hunting camp playground in the Manovo-Gounda Saint Floris National Park (MGSF), which was a vast swath of truly wild Africa.

This park of 17,000 square kilometers in the 1970s and 80s, when I worked there as a wildlife Peace Corps Volunteer, was still a stronghold for western black rhino (Diceros bicornis) and elephants, including an intergrade between bush elephants (Loxondonta africana) and forest elephants (L. a. cyclotis). Gallery forests along the north-south flowing rivers maintained corridors between the southern equatorial forests and the northern Guinean savannas. Mare Gata, a huge water hole in MGSF had over 1,300 hippos basking nose to tail and huge crocodiles feeding off the fish in the super enriched water.

Like Mobutu, who created the first national park in Africa, the Albert National Park, later changed to Virunga National Park, Bokassa created huge national parks in the savanna zone of CAR. Five World Heritage Sites were developed out of Mobutu's park system, and a well-functioning park service, the Institut Zairois pour la Conservation de la Nature (IZCN). Currently, all these World Heritage Sites are classified as In Danger.

Although, ostensibly, these rulers were looked at as conservationists, Bokassa sanctioned and profited from an ivory-exporting business called La Couronne. Most of the supply of ivory for La Couronne came from a northern extension of dense forest around the town of Bangassou along the Ubangi in the east of the country. La Couronne, managed by a Belgian woman and a young Spaniard, obtained a virtual monopoly in 1976 to trade in ivory from President Bokassa, reportedly a shareholder in the enterprise. Here some of the last big tuskers carrying ivory of more than 100 pounds could still be found. In 1977 the official record of elephants killed suddenly jumped to 4,065, from the 1976 figure of 1,420.

It was reported that military trucks were used to transport this ivory to Bangui, the capital and company headquarters, for export to China, Japan, and Hong Kong on major airlines, with the ivory transiting Paris and Antwerp. But as one of the airline officials said: "It's only cargo."

After Bokassa was overthrown in September 1979, La Couronne's ivory business was closed down and, unfortunately, so was wildlife law enforcement. By the end of the year 4,000 elephants were reported killed, with ivory weighing 85 tons. The real number, could be closer to 8,000.

In the spring of 1980 the new government forbade all elephant hunting and stopped all trade in ivory. It failed, however, to convince the people of the value of this new policy since many profited from the perhaps 28,000 elephants killed during the three-year ascendancy of La Couronne.

MGSF was the scene of a different kind of massacre with the same devastating effects. This vast northern savanna Sahel zone was a borderless land and contiguous with Chad and Sudan. For centuries, Sudanese horsemen would leave their scorching dry-season home in Darfur and move south across the Bahr Aouk River into northern CAR, bringing huge herds of zebu cattle. They burned the dry grass ahead of them and soon, out of the black cinders, came succulent green grass for the cattle. Plenty of water remained in the Vakaga, Dongolo, and other mares (dry-season oxbows) for the cattle to drink. The herds were left with herd boys, while the men went off on horseback, carrying huge spears, in search of elephants. Some of these Sudanese formed sultanates, such as the northern CAR town of N'Delé, where the remnants of Sultan al-Senussi's slave fort still remains. As far south as the Ubangi, sultanates were formed and the quarry was people for the Khartoum slave trade. Bangassou, mentioned earlier, was such a town, as was Zemio. The entire eastern half of what is now CAR was emptied by the slave trade.

The horsemen tracked the elephants and would cause panic in the herd by riding and shouting, until they separated a large tusker from the herd. While the elephant valiantly charged the horses in front, a horseman would dash in and drive a huge spear up its anus or into its gut. Another spear or two would open the elephant, and the exhausted pachyderm would die of wounds and trauma. The horsemen went on to finish more of their gristly work and then returned to the corpses to hack out the tusks from the skull. This forgotten hunt is chronicled in watercolor in a book, *La Chasse Oublieé*, by Jean Luc Temporal, the park warden at the time I worked in the park.

The wars in Sudan 1980s replaced the spears with automatic weapons, and the pace of the elephant slaughter picked up rapidly. The hunters became known as the Janjaweed, terrorizing the people of Darfur on behalf of the government of Sudan. They continued to cross into northern CAR until 90 percent of the elephants and 100 percent of the rhino were gone. They now travel further afield, and in March 2010, they devastated up to 650 elephants in northern Cameroon's Bouba Njida National Park. After leaving Cameroon, they hit Zakouma National Park in Chad, killing nine more elephants. They were attacked by park guards, who found thousands of rounds of ammunition, along with uniforms, documents, and phones linking the men to the Sudanese Army. They have made several attempts to reach the last remaining refuge for elephants in CAR, the forest elephants of Dzanga-Sangha, a protected area network in the dense forest of the south that I spent two decades working with the BaAka creating and protecting.

ONE

Peace Corps Training

In the heat of the summer, I went to Auburn University, in Auburn Alabama, for technical training in freshwater fisheries. Auburn was chosen not only due to its well-developed aquaculture program but also because Auburn in the summer was a good place to acclimate to the heat of Central Africa. Here I met the fisheries volunteers I would be serving with. They came from places like Palo Alto, California, Lincoln, Nebraska, and Terryville, Connecticut, a total of 10 that were initiated in the Alabama mud catching tilapia by the tail and learning the fine art of raising them in shallow ponds. We learned about fish sex lives and fish parenting. Tilapia are nest builders and, like bluegill, mouth brooders, meaning that if danger was near, they would suck the eggs or tiny fry into their mouths.

Composting for a garden made sense to me, but putting a compost bin in a corner of a fish pond was new. I was most familiar with brook trout, which need clear, fast mountain streams with little rapids, and grappled with the concept that tilapia like the water green. The compost helps to create an algae bloom, something I thought should be avoided. They are filter feeders and love the soup. By day, photosynthesis by the algae produces oxygen. At night, the algae respiration causes an oxygen depletion, and the

1

next morning you would see hundreds of tiny mouths sucking air until the sun reversed the process, and the oxygen was replenished.

We learned of polyculture, mixed bass and bluegill ponds. The bass feed on the fry of the bluegill, which keeps the pond from getting overcrowded with small stunted bluegill and allows the bass to get plump and feisty. We learned all about stocking rates and sex ratios for maximum production. Stocking with all males was the best for growing fat fish, because the males wouldn't waste valuable energy chasing females. If a farmer had plenty of ponds to produce fingerlings to restock after harvesting, these methods increased yields.

At the end of training, my mother flew down to spend my last weekend in the States with me. It was very strange to see her face in the window of a small Cessna as she taxied in. I almost didn't recognize her as she had never flown in a plane before, let alone a single-prop Cessna. We spent a weekend in a cabin on a lake, rowing around the pond and discussing the events of the past year. We talked about how we learned self-reliance down on the farm and the practical skills of carpentry, animal care, and plain hard work. Because we could work, and had the physical strength and common sense of a Yankee farmer, we could withstand and adapt to any circumstances.

After my mother's visit I began my journey to Bangui. I had a quick trip into Paris between flights, and then a short stop in N'Djamena, Chad. I'll never forget the view from the window in N'Djamena, how the orange glow of the light from the small terminal lit the faces and accentuated the silhouettes of the camo-clad military guard keeping the order of the five passengers who disembarked there.

After the stop in Chad we went back into the night sky for the final hour to Bangui, the capital of CAR. Legend had it that the name Bangui was given to this village on the banks of the Ubangi River by the first whites who made it up the river and asked the Africans, in French, what the name of the village was. The Africans thought that they were pointing to the marijuana plants growing along the banks, which were called *bangui* in Sango, the local language, and this became the name of the village that would become the capital of the French colony of Ubangi-Chari and of CAR. A more sound reckoning of the origins of the name came from the French explorers in 1889 who attempted to explore the Ubangi River but were stymied by the rocky rapids. The name for rapids in Bobangui, another local language, is *bangui*, hence the name. I like the marijuana-plant legend better than the river-rapid origins.

My first glimpse of the Ubangi River was of a moonlit streak of silver through light cirrus clouds, reflecting on a broad curve and lined by flickering cooking fires and larger blazes of dry grass. When it was my turn to go through the door of the plane I felt the blast of hot, humid air and smelled the smoke from dry-season fires and evening meals being cooked over open fires. We filed off the plane and onto the tarmac while heavily armed soldiers made sure no one strayed from the designated route.

The airport was surreal. Huge bugs circled the bright lights that lit the way to the tiny terminal. Across the top of the terminal were the words "Bangui-M'Poko," the airport named for the city and the river bounding Bangui. People hung over the balcony to greet their families and friends, and Peace Corps volunteers, on what would become familiar airport runs, were drinking Mocaf beer and checking out this new batch of recruits below, walking nervously into the unknown.

Another thing I learned from that first night at the Bangui-M'Poko was what a queue, or line, meant in Africa. Instead of an orderly progression to present passports and health cards, there was a general crush toward the narrow passage with everyone reaching over the others waving their passports, some with a 5,000-cfa bill in local currency peeking from the edge of the passport. Then there were the *kota zos,* the important people, who simply barged through and were waved past to waiting vehicles. Not knowing French or Sango, I didn't have to feign ignorance since I was truly naïve to the custom of bribery when the immigration guy dropped broad hints. Seeing that I was a neophyte, he just stamped my passport with the first of many Central African Republic stamps I would receive over the next 30 years.

My next lesson on CAR soil was learning how to negotiate getting my luggage without it disappearing into the darkness. Fortunately, we were not alone and had some experienced volunteers and Peace Corps facilitators helping us through, and we loaded baggage and scared volunteers into the backs of Toyota Land Cruisers while porters shouted for tips, claiming mistreatment for all the work they claimed to have done on our behalf. The trucks roared out, the airport madness faded behind, and we entered the strange world of Bangui by night. The only electric lights were streetlights, while kerosene lanterns burned in front of mud-brick houses. Shadows crowded the dark streets, and tinny music blasted from the wood-planked bars filled with men drinking Mocaf beer. On quieter streets, students read under the streetlights with a frenzied swarm of katydids that became late-night snacks.

We were taken to the center of town to the Protestant Center and passed our first adrenaline-filled, jet-lagged night in CAR. We woke up early the next morning and gathered bleary eyed for our first breakfast of baguettes, greaselike butter, and bowls of coffee with, sweetened condensed milk. As a vegetarian and a careful eater, I tapped the baguette on the edge of the table and rhetorically asked, "is this what I'm supposed to eat for the next two years?"

After breakfast we got back in the truck and went onto the only paved road in the country to our Peace Corps training site in Mbaiki, the capital of the Lobaye Prefecture. With the wind whipping back our long hair, we stood in the back of the Land Cruisers holding on to the tarp frames and watched the panorama of unusual sights go by: President Jean-Bidel Bokassa's residence in Baringo, nine police barriers and barefoot women carrying baskets filled with wood stacked six feet high above their heads. People bathing in streams waved wildly and yelled, *"Munju"* when the truck full of wide-eyed young white people passed by. All vehicles had to slow to 30 kilometers per hour in the village of Bobangui, past the tomb of Barthélemy Boganda, the man considered to be the father of the CAR.

At each police barrier, as our Peace Corps host haggled over paper work with the soldiers looking for a laugh, a shakedown, and a bribe, we watched women in brightly colored cloth wrapped around their bodies carrying pans full of everything from greens to a cow head on their heads and heard the rhythmic heartbeat of Central Africa, which is the sound of a mortar and pestle pounding manioc into flour. The acrid manioc smell that would become so familiar assaulted my nose at this first exposure. Chickens wandered around and picked at the white manioc drying on rocks, adding their own white droppings to the mix, all to be swept up, pounded into flour, mixed with hot water in a pot held between calloused feet, and turned into the staple food, *boule de manioc*, known as *gozo* in the local language.

Manioc, or cassava, was brought to Africa from Brazil by the Portuguese. People grew yams, millet, corn, and other staples, but manioc was manna for the colonists. The plant is easy to grow—a cutting of the stem is stuck in the dirt, and the nodes form roots and a huge starchy tuber which is devoid of nutrients yet is very filling.

This freed the Africans to do more forced labor for the colonists. The palmate leaf, looking quite like marijuana, is part of a great sauce called *ngunza* which is a mix of peanut butter, hot pepper, and dried fish or meat.

Pounding manioc.

Mbaiki–In-Country Training

We young recruits were housed in dormitories at the ISDR (Institut Supérieur de Développement Rural) University in Mbaiki. Mbaiki is the capital of the Lobaye Prefecture. A prefecture is sort of like a state, and the préfet is the governor. ISDR was almost an open-air university, a block structure with ample air circulation. Toilets in the rooms were squatters, with a pull cord to release the water from the tank overhead. At night, on the way back from dinner, huge goliath and rhinoceros beetles circled the lights, and moths of every description flew in circles. Hawk moths dive-bombed. Lights went out at 10 P.M., and reading past that time was done by Aladdin kerosene lamps, until a kamikaze moth would dive down the globe and break the glowing mantle. Before sunrise, roosters would crow and wake up sleep-deprived trainees. I bought a crossbow made by the

BaAka near Mbaiki, and tried unsuccessfully to silence the roosters with the poison-tipped bolts.

We were three months in training at Mbaiki. We "fish" would spend most of the day at the Mbaiki Fish Station, mostly always muddy, slimy-handed, and mostly having a great time. We dug ponds; we drained ponds; we seined fish; we sorted fish by age and sex; we thought like a fish. We named ourselves the *zo ti soussou* (fish people), and built the comradery and friendship that would last well beyond our two years in country.

We all tried to do special projects. Proud of my carpentry skills, I decided to build a holding cage, to hold *alevins* (fingerlings) in a pond while waiting to take them to stock a new pond. I gathered up rough 2x4's, scraps of African mahogany rummaged from the local sawmill, and cut them to length with a dull handsaw. I managed to get nails through the very hard wood, build a frame, and cover it with chicken wire. When I was almost done, my friend Bruce asked me if I had ever built a boat in a basement, meaning that this huge cage wouldn't fit through the door of the workroom in which it was built. Fortunately, mud brick and chicken wire had enough give that I managed to force it out without taking it or the workshop apart.

Our bread was baked and our other food was cooked in a large brick oven with a fire stoked by beautiful red hardwood remnants from the saw-mill. Tony, and other Central Africans who worked for the *stage* (training) would load up a few volunteers for a wood run. Tony became everyone's best friend. He was a young man, a student, handsome and gentle, like an angel coming to the rescue of frustrated volunteers. One day I was just about to kick, stomp, and destroy a motorcycle I was trying to fix that kept flooding, with floats hung up in the carburetor. Tony, a tinkerer with mo-peds and *motos,* calmly came and tapped the carburetor a few times, and the engine revved up right away.

Abel, the principal French teacher, wore bright, embroidered shirts and somehow made total immersion in French fun. We weren't allowed to speak anything but French throughout the day. People got pretty quiet and cheated frequently.

We had our weekend fun. Softball and beer. A pig roast. An occasional African band—Muziki was the top band in CAR at the time, and played at a party. The song at the top of the charts was "Kolnde-na." The key line in the song translated to "Bangui women like to make love to their friends' boyfriends." The cool thing about this song was the play on words in the Sango version. The word *mba* can mean "friend", "buffalo", "to see", or "to have sex." Sango, a tonal language, one word can take on several connotations, depending on the emphasis. The meaning of *mba* was clarified at the end of this line, by saying, *na le ape* (not with eyes).

One of our parties was so good, the guy that managed the potable water tower got drunk and fell into the tank and drowned. He was not discovered for two days, which was enough time for everyone who relied on the tower for their drinking water to get dysentery. The water was shut off while they drained and cleaned the tank. A bucket brigade of healthy volunteers splashed water to wash down and flush the full toilets. Being weakened by dysentery, many, including me, got our first bout of malaria. I remember waking in a cold-sweat delirium, and John, an older volunteer who had been with us since Auburn, was sitting at my side and helping me through.

Somehow we all recovered, and it came time for graduation, getting sworn in, and choosing our posts. The Peace Corps director came from Bangui to Mbaiki, and we all raised our right hands and were officially sworn in as the fish, now clad in our *Zo ti Soussou* tee shirts. After that we had another party and a softball game. One of the volunteers, a large blond guy named Ben, stood drinking a Mocaf in center field, held out a huge bare hand, and caught the last out of the game. We were soon to disperse around the country.

TWO

My First Post–Bocaranga

My first post, Bocaranga, was as far away from Bangui as I could get, in the far northwestern part of the country, close to the border with Cameroon. This is the post that John had started. We became friends, developed a mutual respect, and I was proud to follow in his footsteps.

I choose this area because there were few white people, only a Jesuit mission, with bearded men in long, dark wool robes tied with sashes. There was a working cheese factory, Sarke, and I would ride my 125 Suzuki motorcycle up to buy fresh Camembert. Mail was delivered then, carried on tops of buses filled to the brim with people, sacks of manioc, children, chickens, the roof piled with baggage so high that they would come very close to the tipping point on the rough dirt roads. I got a small fake Christmas tree with 30 ornaments, mailed by my mother in November. It arrived in March with 15 ornaments broken. I could tell that she had sent goodies, chocolate and cookies, as the wrappers were left in the box by the postal workers who helped themselves.

I was given a large cement house in the center of Bocaranga. Across a stretch of wooded savanna emerged the Massif de Yade–an inselberg, which looked like a granite baboon and was considered a sacred mountain. I would walk up the mountain often. There was a maze of woven grass walls to funnel unsuspecting animals, small antelope, cane rats, rock dassies, and the like into deadfall traps-heavy logs set on a thin twig trigger. Rock dassies or hyrax look very much like rodents. Thought to be more closely related to elephants, they have no tail and have blunt hooved feet and tusk-like incisors. They have a top knot of different-colored fur around scent glands, which identify who left the scent and what its status is in the group. One evening I came home with a friend at night and we heard a noise in my house–was it a thief, was it a ghost? It was a barn owl, which are considered by the Central Africans as a bad-juju spirit animal.

I was only the second Peace Corps Volunteer in this post. The volunteer before me, John, had revamped an old fish production station built by the French. In fact, most of the fish posts were in towns or villages that had the remnants of the French fisheries system and had a history of fish culture. The first time I visited the fish station with John, the *sentinel*, or night watchman was roasting a *shisha* rat on a stick over a fire in front of the *magazine* (storehouse). Andre had caught and skewered a good half dozen rats on a stick and was burning the hair off them and roasting these delicacies.

Andre was responsible for pounding cotton seed, gathered from the cotton cooperative in the area, into fish food to be scattered into the ponds to feed the voracious tilapia. The food was supplemented by breaking small phallic termite mounds, banging them together to turn the juicy termites into tilapia flesh. Manioc leaves and sweet potato leaves were ripped up and thrown in for the fish to snack on. Basically, tilapia are easy keepers and well adapted to a more basic form of fish culture.

We were raising *Tilapia nilotica*, a species native to Africa, but not throughout the region. Farmers were encouraged to put some sort of screen, an old pot top riddled with holes, or something in the canal dug from the passing stream to fill the pond with water once ready. This was to try to keep the native *Tilapia zilli* from getting in the pond. *T. zilli* multiplied quickly, filling the pond, leading to overcrowded conditions causing stunting in the fish. It was even more difficult to keep out the walking catfish, *Silurian sp.* They would pull themselves along in the mud from the neighboring streams or swamps on their boney fin rays and help themselves to the tilapia fry.

John had begun an extension program in the region around Bocaranga. I expanded the program, teaching people the fine art of pond digging. Ponds were hand dug near a water source, or into the water table. The ideal pond was about one are (10 meter x 10 meter), about .5 meter deep at the upper, shallow end, lower than the water source so it could be filled, then slopping down to about a meter in depth at the deep end. If too deep, the water would have to be bucketed out, a process called *iri ngu*. And of course, the compost bin in the corner! The soil was mostly clay and held water well, if no roots penetrated the dikes, and burrowing crabs didn't cause a blowout.

Being near a water source or stream, fish ponds were mostly made in the hollow below the villages. Often this was where palms grew that provided sweet palm wine. The flower of the palm was tapped into an old plastic vegetable oil bottle or gourd. After an early morning pond visit, the host farmer would usually offer a liter or ten of palm wine to thank me for my help. In the mornings it was cool and fresh, about as strong as hard cider. It was drunk from a half-gourd or a plastic cup. If you're fussy, you could pick out the floating flies and ants, if not, you just brush them to the far side of the cup as you drink.

Most of the palm wine was from the oil palm, and was generally called *kongoya*. In the dry north, like the Bocaranga area, millet beer, called *bili-bili,* was fermented, usually in a big blackened pot. The actively fermenting brew was ladled out with a half-gourd. This was the Guinness of local beers–*bili-bili* is good for you! *Duma,* another local beverage, was brewed from honey, either harvested in the wild or from huge straw hives set in trees. Some honey was bottled and sold in Cameroon and elsewhere, but the main market was *duma.* In fact, the best way to make a decent subsistence living was selling one form of alcohol or another. *Bako,* the local corn liquor, white lightning, was brewed in 55-gallon (100-liter) barrels, using break-lines from abandoned vehicles as fermenting tubes and a rolled tube of metal roofing to funnel the liquid from the fermentation chamber to a large wine bottle. This wasn't a drink for the fainthearted, but those with little cash wanting the best bang for their *pata* (small change), it was the way to go.

I had several hundred fish farmers in and around Bocaranga, so I couldn't hang around for a wine tasting at every stop, but I'd usually come home with chickens, bananas, or pineapples strapped to my luggage rack. When a new farmer had a new fish pond ready, it would either be stocked with fingerlings from a nearby pond being drained that day, or transported by me in a 30-liter barrel strapped to the luggage rack of my Suzuki. It was quite a motocross challenge balancing a barrel of sloshing fish-filled water down little footpaths to pond side or through the deep sand on some roads.

Although we had an introduction to Sango in our Peace Corps training, the real learning was by total immersion. Unlike the French, the Africans really appreciated and laughed along with me as I struggled with Sango. The French rarely learned Sango and expected the Africans to learn French–*vive la francophonie!* I had a young tutor helping me in the evenings and thought I was picking it up pretty well. So, I thought I'd try it out in the *marché* one Sunday morning. Being a vegetarian, I went looking for eggs. As a Sango newbie, I didn't understand at first the laughter from the vendors, mostly neighbors and friends. I asked for *puru ti kondo*, and evoked lots of laughs. Turns out that eggs are actually *para ti kondo* and *puru ti kondo* means chicken shit!

When it was mango season, I gorged on this orgasmic fruit. Up in the north, it was a bit too dry for manioc, but we ate the *boule* made from millet, and a rare treat, a *boule* made from ripe plantains. Louis Abakar was assigned by the Ministry of Waters and Forests as my counterpart. He was slight, very proper, and wore crisp uniforms. He was an excellent communicator, and together we would ride on my *moto* to meet with fish farmers far and wide!

For some forgotten reason, I had to go to Bangui. It was a two-day ride by motorcycle, and I would spend a night in Yaloké with the American Baptist missionaries. They lived in a compound of 1960's style raised ranch houses, served chocolate chip cookies and a home-cooked, American style meal, and a warm bed for the night. All I had to do was to be on my best behavior and edit my English. The various factions of Baptists and Brethren Frères would accuse each other of sheep stealing. They did have some good health care programs and other development activities, as long as the Africans accepted J.C. as their savior and didn't dance, drink, or have sex. There were few true adherents. Many people would go to church because they liked the singing and the free sardines given to each congregant.

A trip to Bangui involved important Peace Corps business and medical stuff, but mostly cold beer, dancing at the night clubs in Kilometre Cinq. K5 was the African *quartier* under the French regime, with the center of town reserved for French only. This became the area of town where all the action was–great music, dancing, roast chicken and meat cooked on grills along the road, served in a banana leaf with a dash of *piment* pepper.

I began my ride back toward Bocaranga, made my stop in Yaloké, and went on the next day. I was cruising along on a good piece of clay road at about 60 kilometers per hour, rounding a bend with banks along the roadside. There was a dip in the road, and as I veered to avoid it, so did a hunter riding a bicycle coming the other way. We had both swerved in the same direction, so off balance, I careened back, into the hole in the road. I was airborne like Evel Knievel without the talent. The bike went up and I went down, sliding about 20 meters on my back in the hard, gravelly clay. I let out a bloodcurdling scream. The hunter freaked out, thinking that he just killed a *munju*, and he disappeared. I lay on my back and could see the gas running out of the *moto's* tank and knew I had to get it together. I got myself up on two legs, my back bloodied, shirt sticking into my road burns, I lifted the bike onto its kickstand. A bit later, a couple of men came along, and I had them help me straighten the handlebars and push me to start the *moto*, and I headed back down the road toward the mission in Yaloké. My back and arms now swollen, I rode rigidly, and slowly. At the mission, they cleaned my wounds as I passed out. The next day, I was back on a truck, my bent *moto* tied in, en route to Bangui. So, more medical attention, more cold beer.

Now in Bangui, I decided to go on an Easter vacation, to the town of Bambari, on the other side of the country, to do a river trip with my friend Liza. Liza was a TEFL (teaching English as a foreign language) volunteer. Bambari is a large town on the banks of the Ouaka River. The Ouaka is a tributary of the Ubangi, and we thought we'd get a pirogue, (dugout canoe) and head south with the flow of the river, to end our voyage back in Bangui. Liza, a tall, stately woman from near Roanoke, Virginia, spoke with a true blue Southern accent. I rode to Bambari on the top of a big lorry full of sheep making its way to Chad. At night, I wrapped myself in the dirty tarp on the big ledge above the pungent sheep, and marveled at the stars. Owls and nightjars would pop up off the road, where they huddled and hunted.

Even in a big town like Bambari, it wasn't hard to find the home of the tall *munju* woman.

I went the next morning with Liza's helper and we bought a five-meter-long dugout with two paddles and a pole. Normally, especially going upstream, one person holds a paddle as a rudder in the stern, while the other walks as far out on the bow as possible, plants the pole in the muddy bottom, braces it against his body and simply walks back toward the stern, pushing the boat along. We packed up two weeks' worth of food, iodine tablets to purify water, a tent, etc., and pushed off from the banks of Bambari.

Witnessing Africa by river gives a new perspective. As we drifted silently along the banks, the forest slipping by on both sides, white throated blue swallows perched on snags sticking above the brown water, and a fin foot (bird) ran across the surface to flee. An occasional De Brazza's monkey would call and dart through the trees, and azure blue malachite kingfishers streaked along keeping just ahead of our boat. People in Bambari assured us that it would take about one week to reach the confluence of the Ouaka and the Ubangi. A day out, I called to a fisher and asked how many days down river; he estimated eight. Every day I would ask someone we saw, and each added a day. I thought we must be going backward! We'd see the occasional hippo, and hear the splash of crocodiles startled by our passing.

About three days out, I scratched some grass cuts on my right knee. I cleaned it well with alcohol and put a dressing on it. But it grew. It formed a hard core, a typical tropical ulcer. When we stopped, I would heat water to make hot compresses in hopes that it would drain. My body temperature began to rise. I hung off the side of the boat to cool down. We stopped at a domed hunting camp with smoke filtering through the grass covering. We asked to come in. I lay down next to the fire, and fell into a deep sleep.

These kind people feed us *gozo* and fresh fish, and we reluctantly left the warmth of their hospitality and went back to our pirogue.

By now my fever was reaching 106 as we drifted on. Finally, we saw a mission town at the confluence of the Ouaka and Ubangi. It was in sight, but we could not get there. In this early dry season, sand bars confused channels, and water flowed in swirls, declining to two inches. I tried to push the pirogue with my good leg, while Liza, with the bowline over her shoulder, dragged us through the shallow water. We were exhausted and camped on the sandbar, with only cold *mambele* (fermented manioc eaten by travelers) to eat. I lay in our tent, pitched to fend off the mosquitos, hallucinating deep thirst, but had the conditioning to fill a water bottle from the river, add halazone tablets, and wait twenty minutes, before quenching this insatiable thirst.

Finally, the next morning, we made our way to the French Catholic mission. Because of my high fever, they put me in a breezy palm leaf thatched hut outside the main building. The only antibiotics they had were some tetracycline, which couldn't touch this infection. Liza worked with them to fire up their radio to call in to the Peace Corps in Bangui. The Peace Corps nurse, Nurse Friedle, a young Belgian woman, would be on a small plane within two days. The missionaries had people go the break down termite mounds on the landing strip and cut the tall grass to make way for the very rare plane to land.

While I lay in my delirium, a large older African woman, with a scarf in her hair, pushed back the palm leaf door and said, "I can heal you," a scene that I can picture clearly to this day. Being incoherent, I was not receptive, and this is one of my greatest regrets.

The Cessna landed, Friedle and the pilot came, and we loaded into the small plane. I brought my paddle with me. Off to Bangui. A truck met us and we went to the only private clinic in Bangui, the Schweb Clinic. This, like so many businesses in Bangui, was Lebanese owned. The next day, they paraded the best of the Bangui doctors by my bedside. One insisted that the two marks on my knee must be a spider bite, so he loaded me up with antivenom. Another prescribed steroids. I spent five weeks on my back in this clinic, and no one thought to take a culture to see what the infection actually was.

At this time, we had no Peace Corps country director. The PC doctor had been psychovaced, sent home because of a mental breakdown. The brand new associate director, Jim, didn't want to appear weak and send me out of the country. Finally, he requisitioned a seat on a flight to Paris, we painfully made it to the airport, and then we were told that there was no room. Instead of insisting, we returned again to the Schweb Clinic. By now, my leg was like a giant Stay-Puft marshmallow, and I was delirious with fever. Finally, Jim realized through Liza's insistence that I had to get serious medical attention very, very soon. John and another volunteer carried my stretcher onto the next plane. Six seats were reclined, and the stretcher was secured and a drape drawn. Friedle accompanied me. When we landed in Paris, an ambulance met us at the plane and I was taken to the American Hospital. They got me off all the funky medications they put me on in Bangui, let the infection form abscesses, took a culture, and found that I had a massive strep infection in my leg! I could see the chestnut blossoms out the window as the anesthesiologist administered her magic and my body fell away. The operation took hours, and drained seven kilos of puss from my leg.

By now, I was so traumatized, I needed anesthesia so that they could change the bandages. My leg was opened from hip to calf. They told me that the Peace Corps had wanted me to go the military hospital in Germany, but they feared that I would not make it. The head doctor in Paris said that likely they would have cut the other way and amputated the leg. I had a seven-week vacation at the American Hospital in Paris. We decided that my next trip would be west, across the Atlantic, instead of south across the Sahara, and I went home. Initially, we thought that after a three-month recovery period, I would be back in CAR, but I had my worst case of malaria two months in, and decided to stay stateside until the next round of recruits were ready to make their way to Bangui.

I came back to Connecticut and enrolled in a master's program in Ornithology at Southern Connecticut State University under the tutelage of Nobel Proctor. During the winter at home, I did my course work for my master's and would finalize my fieldwork and dissertation back in CAR. I had already begun compiling a bird list including the status of each species in the country as well as habitat associations, and I was determined to finish. This was my maximizing philosophy: I loved birding, was doing the work, so why not use this time back home to tack on a degree?

The summer of 1978, I was back with the new group of fish in Mbaiki, then to a new post in Boganangone. I was now a Lobaye boy, *Zo ti Soussou*. Jim was still on as associate director, with a little more experience under his belt, and a little nervous about a lawsuit, which I was not inclined to pursue. But sensing the guilt, he felt he owed me one. I asked to be transferred to the Wildlife Program in the northern parks, after one year in Boganangone. He agreed.

It was during my second post that I kept a journal full of passionate, perhaps naïve thoughts, which I now read with a smile on my face. What follows are my original writings, bracketed by my current thoughts, looking back 35 years on what I would now say to that young man about his observations.

THREE

Back in the CAR—Second First Impressions

Why are there stars? To comfort us when feeling alone, giving us company in our universal home.

To let us wonder about other beings sharing the universe with us.

To let us expand out of ourselves into the vastness of creation.

To let us feel big when feeling small. And the opposite.

Stars are there to humble us when we feel we're the lords of the universe. When we feel we're all that is, stars are there to remind us that we're part of the greater whole, a cell in the universal body itself.

Stars are there to give us a glimpse of boundlessness, to help us unbind ourselves. To give us points of light in the darkness and to guide us on our universal path.

And to give us points of connection around the world. As I lay on my back on my grass mat in the Central African Empire, I saw the same Orion overhead as I saw in Cheshire, Connecticut. And the Big Dipper hung above the northern horizon pointing to Polaris around which the heavens turn. Through the rain-washed, pollution-free African atmosphere, and the stars may glow clearer, the Milky Way like a thin dusting of snow in the cool night, a trail of light traversing the universe. And the trail leads my mind anywhere I think to be. Lying there on my back, I could beam my being to any mountain, any shore where I watched these stars before.

And I was being right there in the beginning of the rainy season, as shades of browns become greens and my gardens grew again. In my dry season travels, I filled my pockets with seeds of trees, fruits, and flowers to create an African arboretum.

Having no guidebook to name African flowers and trees, my creativity was freed to call them what I wished. "A rose is a rose is a rose—by any other name it would smell as sweet!"

Loving care for plants and animals wasn't a trait I'd found flourishing among Africans. Entrenched in African tradition, plants and animals are threats, tools, and food. From grasshoppers to gorillas, animals were given by God to be used by people. African reverence for plants and animals is based on one reality. Their lives depend on them.

Forest, field, and savanna provided food and shelter. There was little of the artificial separation of people and the earth that exists in a modern society. People are personally involved in the process of collecting and preparing food. Food comes directly from the earth, not prepackaged, preserved, and plasticized.

Keeping of pets was a rarity among Central Africans. Dogs were kept to help in hunting and were generally kept hungry and half wild. A dog looking for food or a warm place by the fire more often got kicked than petted.

The combined effects of traditional society, slave trading, colonialization, and Westernization have created a classed social structure. Through traditional conflicts and slaving one tribe exploited another. Europeans exploited all Africans. The slave trade forced people to flee their homes; colonials and missionaries robbed the richness of ancient African cultures. Patronizing colonials partitioned the people into *kota zo's* (big people) and peasants. Foreign French educational systems formed a marginally educated upper class of a few, while failing to provide a broad-based education for the people. Capitalism created a money-hungry merchant class, mostly Muslim, peddling plastic shoes and rejected Western clothes worn until ragged by the Africans. Condescending *kota zo's* patronized the peasants and everyone was caught somewhere between traditionalism and Westernism. Imagine the confusion of being forced from Stone Age to Atomic Age in a few decades!

The country's motto of *Zo ayeke zo*, on monuments in every village square, which means People are people, all people are equal, was rarely a reality. My being white here made people automatically expect me to act as their patron-boss. But as the sweat of my brow mixed with theirs, as we worked our gardens, when they saw the rare sight of blisters and calluses on white hands, and when they felt my love as I opened my hands and heart to them, they too opened to me and shared the beauty of being there together, sharing the seasons, sun and stars and the love of life that truly makes us all one.

2015

There's still a bit of the rosy-glassed 23-year-old spirit that has stuck with me. I named my daughter, Deva, after the nature spirits and my older son, Orion, for that constellation that has always brought me home.

Zo kwe zo, zo ayeke zo–All People are One–CAR motto.

I've learned more about the relationship between people, plants, and animals. I walked on elephant trails through the forest with the BaAka Pygmies almost every day for almost 10 years. I was doing my PhD work on lowland gorillas, while establishing a conservation program across the Congo Basin. Plants are used for medicine, some ingested for their curative properties, but more often, certain plants are woven into bands and worn as amulets, anklets, or around the midsection for the spiritual protection or value they bring.

While conducting vegetation surveys in my study area, I asked Mekama, a *tuma*, or renowned hunter among the BaAka, what the bands on his ankles were for. At first he pulled some vines and, when we reached a clearing, sat down. He began rolling the vines together against his thigh, making a tight, rope-like band. He instructed me to roll up my pant leg. He tied one on my right ankle, and explained that this gives us good luck in the hunt and protects us from being injured by dangerous animals. While in the forest, I and my team found lots of animals and never got stomped by an elephant or mauled by a gorilla, so it worked. On my left ankle, he tied another band. This was for fertility. Two weeks later, Deva was conceived. I am a firm believer in BaAka medicine.

I was privileged to live and work with the BaAka and was able to glimpse the life of forest foragers. The forest provides the cultural, spiritual, and physical needs of the BaAka, and they have a deep reverence for the forest. The *jengi*, or forest spirit, guides their life in the forest and only appears in an intact forest. The BaAka are, by nature, conservationists and were partners in establishing the Dzanga-Sangha program.

In my first years in CAR, I was blind to ethnic tension, and the Sango language seemed to unite the 70-plus ethnic groups in the country. Sango was a tribal tongue, became a trade language, and the national language.

Zo kwe zo. Then I learned that the Sudanese drivers of the slave trade and hunters of elephants and people, called the Aouke River, which divides Sudan and CAR, Bahr Bakoya—the river of baboons. This implied that those living south of this river were subhuman and fair game for the slave trade.

During the term of André Kolingba, a Yakouma from the east of the country, his presidential guard (all Yakouma of course) committed excesses, and suddenly all Yakouma were enemies of all others. Neighbors rose against neighbors in Bangui, and many died.

The most recent, and more flagrant, case followed the coup d'état of 2012, which toppled President François Bozizé and brought in an Islamic group calling themselves Seleka. Seleka means "coalition," and various rebel groups banded together, supported by Chad and others, to push Bozizé out and establish an Islamic state. Most of the fighters for the various Seleka factions were basically mercenaries from Chad and other points north, and the coalition had only one goal in common—taking power. Not having been paid for their efforts, the fighters took to looting, raping, and killing Central Africans. In reaction, the largely non-Islamic Central Africans formed the anti-Balaka ("anti-machete") and fought back against the unorganized Seleka, and began an ethnic cleansing of all Muslims in CAR. Neighbors, merchants, shopkeepers, market women—people of several generations in CAR, no longer holding ties with Chad, Sudan or wherever their families originated—were killed, beaten, and finally moved en mass by the U.N. to Chad. *Zo kwe zo.*

FOUR

Boganangone, My Little Savanna home.

1978

"*B*arrao Richard," (Hello, Richard) the village chief said, termite wing hanging in the hair of his chin. He extended one hand to shake; in the other was in a metal bowl.

"*Mo ye ti te?*" (You want to eat?) he said, extending the bowl containing a tangle of tired termites trying vainly to climb the enameled slopes. A crunch and another dozen lacey wings landed in the pile at his feet.

"*Oh, no merci. Mbi te niama ape.*" (No thanks. I don't eat meat.)

"*Banga ti nye?*" (Why not?)

"*Banga ti nzapa a tene na mbi ti te niama ape.*" (Because God told me not to eat meat.)

This had excused me from not only termites but also caterpillars, katydids, and grasshoppers. The virtues of vegetarianism. But it's far out that these people partook in such plentiful protein resources. People adapted to their environment–the grasslands. Houses, baskets, mats, and hats made of grass, and all the succulent savanna food sources abounded.

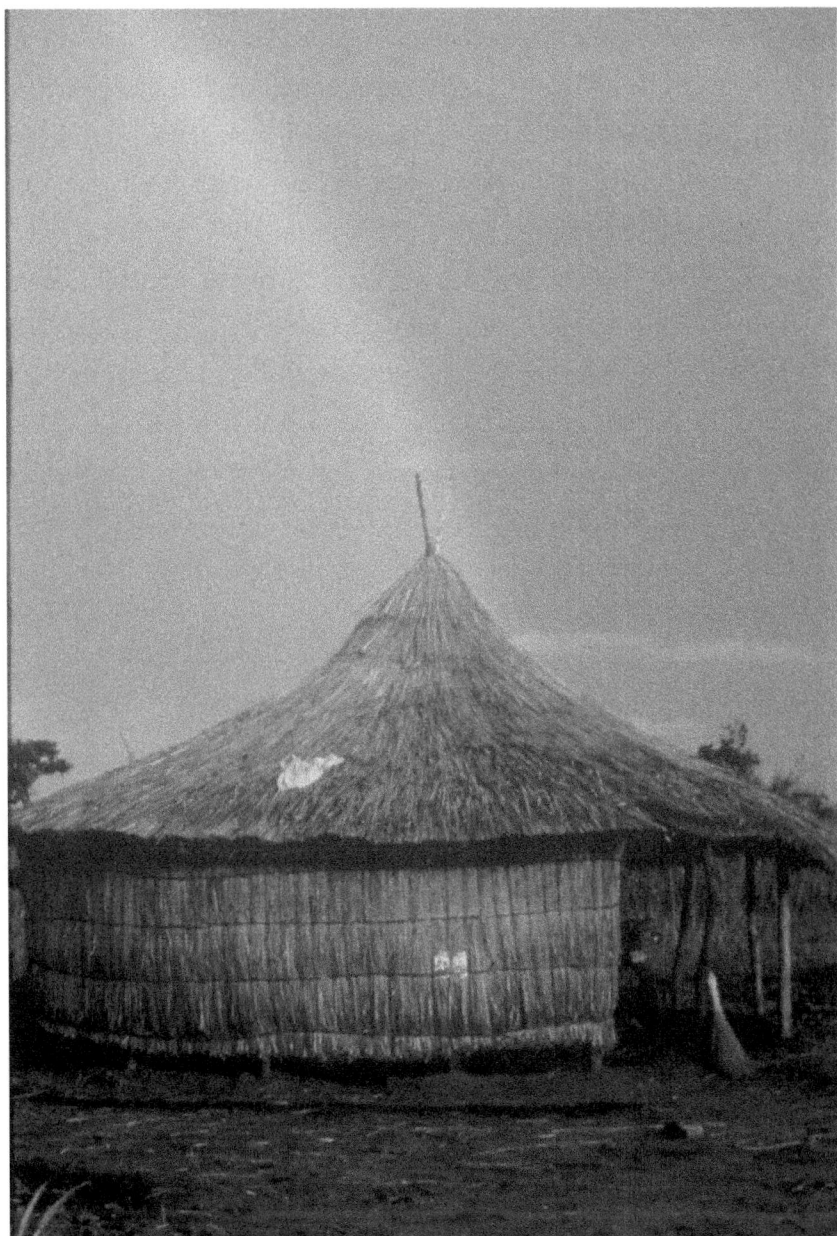

My *paillote* home in Boganangone.

People living in grass houses shouldn't play with fire. But I liked to watch the golden sparks fly into the black sky and disappear into the darkness. Thus, the grass I had cut in the last few days gave its light back to the sun again. From sun we come to sun we go. And the cleared space around my house and *paillote* (round grass hut) grew; providing protection and buffering the blaze of the sweeping savanna fires that brighten the night. Sweeping, leaping, reaching, and releasing the pyromaniac's pantomime in pastel. The aurora tropicalis.

I'm not the only one who risked ruin from the blaze. Everything from gophers to grasshoppers made its home of grass. And when the blaze began, everyone from hawks to humans hungrily hunted the animals as they fled their fiery homes. The golden reds of fire tones reflected bronzy browns of body tones as men and mice and the fire and the night dance to the reflecting rhythms of life tones.

And my grass house still stood.

"Step right up, folks–right here on this path in the middle of this manioc field right here somewhere in the middle of Africa–the greatest show on earth!"

"See the daring dung beetles walk backwards on their forelegs while their other four legs roll a ball of bull dung like a circus seal with a beach ball. What fate, what karma leads a soul's reincarnation into the life of a dung beetle?"

However, there are more species of dung beetles on earth than almost any other life form, each feeding on different dung. We certainly live in a world full of dung!

"And there to your right–among the purple, green and maroon manioc (cassava) stems–look closely and you'll see, shimmying up stems with vice-like grips of its three opposing digits on each of its four scaly legs, prehensile tail tightly coiled like a South American monkey, doing dances, looking like an all-in-one, does-everything appliance that even changes color—yes, folks, the amazing ever-adaptable chameleon!"

"See the clever little gray-bodied, red-tailed, snap-tail gecko scamper across the path. Red tail to divert possible predators from vital areas. The pursuing predator, excited by the red tail, attacks. The tail neatly severs, leaving the predator with a bony, wiggly mouthful, while the tailless little lizard darts into the brush."

Anyway, such were a few wayside attractions while walking with fish farmers to the ponds.

Any excuse to dance would do. Even to celebrate the first anniversary of His Imperial Majesty Jean Bidel Bokassa, emperor. On December 4, people from miles around gathered in area centers, mostly clad in bright colored cotton clothes with patterns depicting the emperor and empress along with Mamans Décorées, women honoring their country by having five or more children, to celebrate the occasion with parades and dancing, drinking of corn liquor and drumming, singing and more dancing. Back snapping, shoulder shaking, circling, chanting, a cyclone centered on the heartbeat of drums. Bronze bodies tinged red with dust, streaked with sweat gleaming in noontime sun, shimmering scarlet in sunset colors, rising with the moon, spinning with the earth, pouring right on through the next day's rain. Two thousand people dancing into themselves and out of themselves. Each doing their own dance around the same drum.

Fête and parade honoring Emperor Bokassa.

Mamans Décorées

And the beans were hanging heavily on the vines growing up my house poles, my squash blooms yellow, zinnias surround my *paillote* like pastel stardust, like little nectar-flavored butterfly ice cream cones.

2015

I eventually relaxed my vegetarian ways, and stopped lying about God, which made me an infinitely better guest, and allowed me to share in some rare delicacies. As an honored guest, I sampled treats such as Gabon viper, tripe, porcupine, rhinoceros beetle larvae, caterpillars, an occasional monkey, and many a goat and chicken. With manioc and a warm Mocaf, what could be better? I did turn down any meat from protected species, such as elephant trunk and gorilla, as well as illegally hunted bush meat. In addition to the hunting of elephants for ivory and rhino for their horn, the bush meat trade (wildlife illegally harvested for sale) is the leading cause of biodiversity loss in Africa.

My first post, Bocaranga, was as far from Bangui as I could get. Boganangone, in the south-center of the country, was a tiny village of 400 Gbaya-Bofi people, with no missions, no other white people. This gave me the opportunity to experience a fairly traditional life and be part of the family around the fire at night, telling stories under the stars. My nearest Peace Corps neighbor, Phil, lived in the regional capital of Boda, 60 kilometers south, and Rob lived in Yaloké, on a major road, 90 kilometers north. I was on the road less traveled.

FIVE

Fish Farming in Central Africa

1978

It was early November in the Central African Empire and the termites rose in the air. Rising, circling, swirling in guided confusion, as they emerged winged for the first time from their cavernous, fungus-farming home in the ground. Unfolding their clear, new appendages in the wind, they focused on the sun, and in a rush and perfect madness their maelstrom ascended. And everything from hammerkops to hornbills hovered hungrily seeking the succulent swirling insects. Notched-tailed black kites by the hundred maneuvered mouthful after beaks full. Swallows swooped and dove. A pair of trumpeter hornbills simply sat on the top branch of a tree taking enormous beak bites of air filled with the tantalizing termites. Black shoulder kites and even peregrines took up this circle game.

Children hurried down paths with close-woven baskets to trap their share. The grass domes dotted the landscape built over termite mounds, catching the emerging masses to be collected and consumed like candy by the handful or crunchily cooked.

Back in August and September whole villages would disappear into the forest to find fat caterpillars bursting juicy with every bite tickling the palate with all those little legs.

Most caterpillars managed to mature into butterflies that would beautifully, silently, dancing clap colors on the breeze. Such variety–from midnight blue to blazing red, some in striking contrasts, some looking leaf-like in their camouflage. And all as yet undestroyed by DDT or other pesticide-peoplecide poisons.

As I walked from my little fish station up the path through six-foot-high savanna grass, seed heads in maroons and greens hung heavily in the breeze. The gull-like call of a black kite caught my ear, and I stopped on a hilltop to look back across the waving sea-like, sun-rich savanna. I saw the little valley veiled in a cool canopy forest where my fish ponds lay. Across the rolling green hills I saw the contrasting brown of the grass houses of the Mbororo people. They are a nomadic Muslim Fulani group, herding long-horned zebu cattle through the savanna. The women would stride into town barefoot, brightly clad, balancing gourds of milk on their braided heads. The circling chorus of hawks continued, contrasted against the clouds that were building in the east.

At the top of the path was my home. As I walked up the path, the yellow browns of the round grass roof of my *paillote* rose above the surrounding savanna. I added airy grass walls and roll-away bamboo curtain windows and soon I was living in the round. I slept in a red mud brick house with a grass roof behind my *paillote*. The house had two rooms: a kitchen, and my sleeping and living space with large double-hung wooden windows opening to the savanna sunrise. Also I had a round, woven grass-enclosed hole-in-the-ground *cabinet* (latrine) out back. It's all very unobtrusive here in this sea of grass.

It was so organic; in fact, it was actually decomposing around me. My roof leaked; termites were eating the pole roof rafters; the rain that blew in from the east was eating my wall with the wooden sunrise windows. So I added an outer wall of woven grass to protect the mud bricks from eroding away and I prepared my *paillote* for habitation.

I had a three stone cooking fireplace in front of the kitchen, green beans climbed the poles supporting my roof; flowers were all around, and newly planted palms and mangos for future fruit and shade. I had hills of squash, cantaloupe, and peas, and out back a garden of carrots, kale, corn, beets, and tomatoes. Daikon radishes were the favorite of my elderly male neighbors who believed that they were aphrodisiacs! All were watered by the reliable rains.

These late rainy season "roads" were almost impossibly impassable. But in true dedication as a fisheries extension agent I took up the daily challenge because "the *soussou* must get through." So early each morning, fortified by papaya puree, banana, and citronella tea, I donned my Sears and Roebuck black rubber knee-high boots, my full blue Kelty rain suit, blue helmet, and leather gloves, mounted my blue 125cc Suzuki motorcycle, and spread the *soussou* word from village to village. And there was mud and puddles of indeterminable–until I fell in–depth and ten-foot grass hanging heavy with the night's rain over the "road." So I did head fakes to dodge the grass's wet slaps in the face and maneuvered my *moto* through and around the holes, termite mounds and sand.

And usually I managed to meet my fish farmer friends. We talked in Sango of the wonders of fish farming and walked in the sunshine to see their ponds. All ponds were hand-dug, and I stocked them with *Tilapia nilotica* fingerlings raised at my fish station and transported in a barrel strapped to the luggage rack on my motorcycle. Try riding on deep sandy roads with 30 liters of water and fish sloshing behind you! From there, with lots of encouragement and a bit of work and six months' time, they harvest. And soon there'll be a pond for every person and a *poisson* on every plate.

Later, I hung out in my hammock strung from a circle pole to the center pole of my *paillote* taking a siesta, listening to the wind rustling my roof and the sounds of the village. Children playing, baby crying, mortar and pestle pounding, rooster crowing, all subdued in the distance, and I drifted into dreams.

Duti nzoni, Cheshire
Nzapa bata ala.

Rest well, Cheshire
God guard you.

2015

The backbone of the fisheries program that Phil, Rob, and the others fostered were the Central African fisheries agents, particularly enthusiastic villagers that we trained as extension agents throughout our regions. They, of course, spoke the local languages and translated the language of fish farming to our clients. We also became good friends. We played Huit Américain (crazy eights) and drank warm beer and palm wine. They added a grounded dimension to the program, and continued for a while after the Peace Corps Volunteer left.

François, from Boda, went with me on my first road trip to Bayanga, to show me the way and to see Bayanga for the first time himself. Kpanou Jean Bosco, a young man who worked at my fish station in Bogangone also asked to come with me to Bayanga. I told him to ask his mother, she agreed, and off he went. He became my assistant in my field work on gorillas and took part, soup to nuts, in the development of the Dzanga-Sangha Program. As a grassroots guy, making a tremendous contribution to conservation, he was awarded the Goldman Prize for Conservation Achievement.

Fisheries agent, *Zo ti Soussou*, François.

Jean Bosco, Clements and family, Boganangone.

Baba George, a very fit agent in Boda, contracted an infection as I did, but had little access to good medical care. Phil and I did what we could, but we certainly couldn't arrange a medevac to Paris. He died. I lived with a big scar. I'm not sure how sustainable the fisheries program was in the long run. The theory was that fish farmers would pay the agents to help them via proceeds from their harvests. In reality, once the Peace Corps left, as when the French left, the program largely died. The Peace Corps rehabilitated old French fish stations. Perhaps they'll be resurrected again. Although I'm sure that ponds still exist and people still harvest fish, most are likely abandoned in the bush. Once the stipend from the Peace Corps ended, so did the work of the agents. Frankly, much of the initial success of the program was having a visit from the white guy on the motorcycle. It was exciting, something different, a touch of the wider world, good connections. Give a person a fish, they eat for a day, teach a person to fish, visit on a motorcycle, and they eat for two years.

Boda became a major battlefield between the Seleka and the anti-Balaka. It was a significant diamond area, so it attracted many Muslim diamond merchants. The Seleka were brutal. Jean Bosco's mother, an elderly woman selling *duma* for extra money, had her knee kicked backward by Seleka shaking her down for her few profits. Her sister and niece had their throats slit like goats. Jean, then living in Bangui, found a rare ride to Yaloké, then walked the 90 kilometers through a bush trail to rescue his mother from Boda and carried her out to Bangui. *Zo kwe zo.*

SIX

The Round of Births

1978

It had come to pass in the village of Boganangone that a child was born unto Celements Zongehina (Medicine Woman) and Richard Sera Sora (Heart Star), and he will bear the name of his spiritual father. This universal being was brought through her body into my hands at sunrise May 6 in the round of my *paillote* into the round of births again. This brown Baya baby being, was born into this earth to grow and (perhaps) liberate Africa with universal love.

Many questions of conceptions of continuity filled my mind. Are our personal realities created by our consciousness and projected onto a screen of physical experience? Do physical forms cease to exist or become remodeled as our point of projection shifts? Is reality like a sand castle formed, destroyed, and continually re-formed by constantly changing creative consciousness? Are we all apparitions or extensions of our consciousness created to fulfill love or karma? How does our creative consciousness intermingle to form the labyrinth of our physical existences?

As I traveled this earth open to love, my extended spiritual family gathered around me forming an international wedding ring of universal love.

Clements.

And now the story of "The Night of the Caterpillar."

I had just extinguished the flame of my kerosene lamp, its glow melting into the darkness of a moonless night. With a sigh I put away the thoughts of the day and prepared the way of dreams. As I drifted I heard a calling from outside my *paillote*. I rose to a solemn circle of village chiefs and a story of a sorcerer's spell and the *sioni chenille* (poisoned caterpillars). They wanted my help. We got into the Peace Corps Toyota pickup, here temporarily for a major fish transport, and proceeded across the village. I shut off the headlights and darkness rushed in around us broken by the wailing of women and the red reflections of fires and silhouetted shadows of milling people against mud brick walls. The crowd parted as we walked through. I stooped through the low entrance of the house, and my eyes adjusted to the firelight, amid the smells of smoke and vomit. I focused on an old lady, face swollen, convulsing in a corner. In another corner a child in coma. In all seven people in various states of consciousness lay around the room. Pulse and respiration present but slow in all.

"Poisoned caterpillars? They ate poisoned caterpillars—water, get them water, help them drink, vomit."

"We've done that already—we must transport them to another sorcerer. We've sent a runner. He's ready."

Well, my emergency medical training course said that, once you've done all you can, transport the patient to the nearest medical facility. The nearest and only medical facility happened to be this sorcerer and, who knows, he might have had an age-old antidote, some surefire caterpillar cure. So we made stretchers of grass mats and one by one carried them to the truck. Each poisoned person was sitting propped against a well person until there were 20 people packed like sardines in the open pickup. Another four in the cabin. And off we went to a village 35 kilometers away on a road no better than a streambed, truck body bouncing on the axle with every bump, five kilometers an hour through the night. Animals darted in the darkness, eyes reflecting the headlights. We arrived at midnight and wove our way through palm trees and mud brick homes directed by the sound of the drums of the special medicine dance prepared by the sorcerer. The entire village participated in this magical medicinal maelstrom to dance away the devil possessing these people. We unloaded them on the grass within the glow of the flames. The medicine man administered his herbs; we all held hands in a healing circle around the people; the dancers danced on. Each drumbeat burning away blockages. Life's energy current chanting, circling higher and higher, rising with the sparks taking our places among the stars. Dancing to the universal heartbeat, dancing into our hearts, dispelling darkness, and directing healing light.

Dancing eagles around the sun
Giving our colors with every turn
Each round closer lessons learned
Each round closer veils burned.
Dancing eagles into the sun
Into our hearts merging one
Into the white light we return.

Our colors filled the sky and merged into the rising sun. I took my leave. Within the next few days all but the old lady returned home to Boganangone. By day fields are farmed, manioc pounded into flour. By night come the drums and dancing. A child was born; an old lady died in the perfect balance of life.

Sera Sora.

2015

I always suspected that the incident was due to pesticide poisoning, possibly something used on cotton. Large amounts of pesticides banned in most of the world end up in third-world countries, either used on crops, or dumped for a fee to rid them from our own backyards. These toxic waste dumps in developing countries may contain more than 500,000 tons of old and unused pesticides that have been banned or expired, and according to the Food and Agriculture Organization (FAO), threaten the environment and health of millions of people. It is estimated that 100,000 tons are in Africa. This lethal legacy includes aldrin, chlordane, DDT, dieldrin, endrin, and heptachlor which all have been banned in many countries. As the pesticides deteriorate, they may form by-products, sometimes more toxic than the original substance.

The World Health Organization (WHO) estimates that more than 1 million people are affected by exposure to pesticides worldwide, causing 20,000 deaths annually. According to the FAO, these forgotten stocks are not only a hazard to people's health, they also contaminate water and soil. Leaking pesticides can poison a very large area, making it unfit for crop production.

The cost of cleanup and disposal of Africa's obsolete pesticide stocks is estimated at $250 million, thus, cleanup efforts have been slow. An FAO inventory of toxic sites in 39 African countries found that of 48,081 tons of chemicals reported, just 2,838 tons had been destroyed.

In 2001, 122 countries have signed the Stockholm Convention on Persistent Organic Pollutants, banning 12 of the most dangerous compounds. The Global Environmental Facility, managed by the World Bank, United Nations Environment Programme, and the United Nations Development Programme will finance the implementation of the convention.

SEVEN

The Sorcerer's Revenge

1978

It was February in Boganangone, Central African Empire, and the shadow of a black kite flowed across parched baked sand, up and over the contours of my *paillote*, over the waves of brown savanna grass, keeled tail guiding it through the ocean of air and sun. It seems that all creations, as all colors, have their complements and/or contrasts, like hawks floating in air and fish flying in water.

And was there a connection between the full-moon African earth tremors that shook the continent to its core that night and the heart energy of the African people seeking release and expression to reform their society as the earth rumbles to re-form itself? It was a time that the surface tension could no longer hold down what was going on inside. As pent-up earth energy woke people in the night and brought houses tumbling down, so the release of people power in Africa was shaking the structure that had shackled the society for so long. The earth had always provided for the people of Africa, and the earthquake power provided a complement to the creative people energy. And you can't stop an earthquake.

Now the story of Pandora's proverbial poisoned pineapple that was peacefully resting in my kitchen with just a mere mud brick *mur* (wall) between us. Just that afternoon the pineapple reached ripeness in the rich African sun nestled in its pointed green leaves in a row of pineapple plants lining the *legue* (road) separating my "property" from my neighbor's. What set this pineapple apart from the others was a stick with a bunch of grass tied to one end and stuck in the ground next to it. This grass was "medicine" to protect the pineapple from being picked by the people on the path. Following the old proverb that good pineapples make good partners, my good neighbor presented it to me. I planned on pineapple for dinner. Then some friends came over, saw the pineapple had been picked, and placed it in my kitchen. Being good friends, they proceeded to prescribe all the evil that would befall one who eats a pineapple protected by a fetisher's "medicine." I said as long as I thought good thoughts no evil could touch me. But I decided on papaya for dinner. And then the phantom pineapple lurked in the next room. My kerosene lamp flame flickered in the wind, casting huge dancing demon shadows on my walls. Every rustle of the wind in my grass roof was the pineapple. Every lizard scampering across my wall I turned to see.

Every sound was the pineapple growing. It was growing so big it was going to break down the wall and get me. I woke at dawn determined to have a pineapple *petit dejeuner* (breakfast). I held my knife like a cross to Dracula. I pierced its heart. It bled sweet and sticky on my hands. I ate the whole thing. And my walls still stood despite earthquakes and poisoned pineapple.

The Boganangone Bumbi ti Bassin, the fish pond team, was in action. About 20 people who, if they're promised *bako* and *gozo*, corn liquor and manioc, will get their shovels and dig you a pond. And songs and laughter rose with the smoke of pond-bank cooking fires.

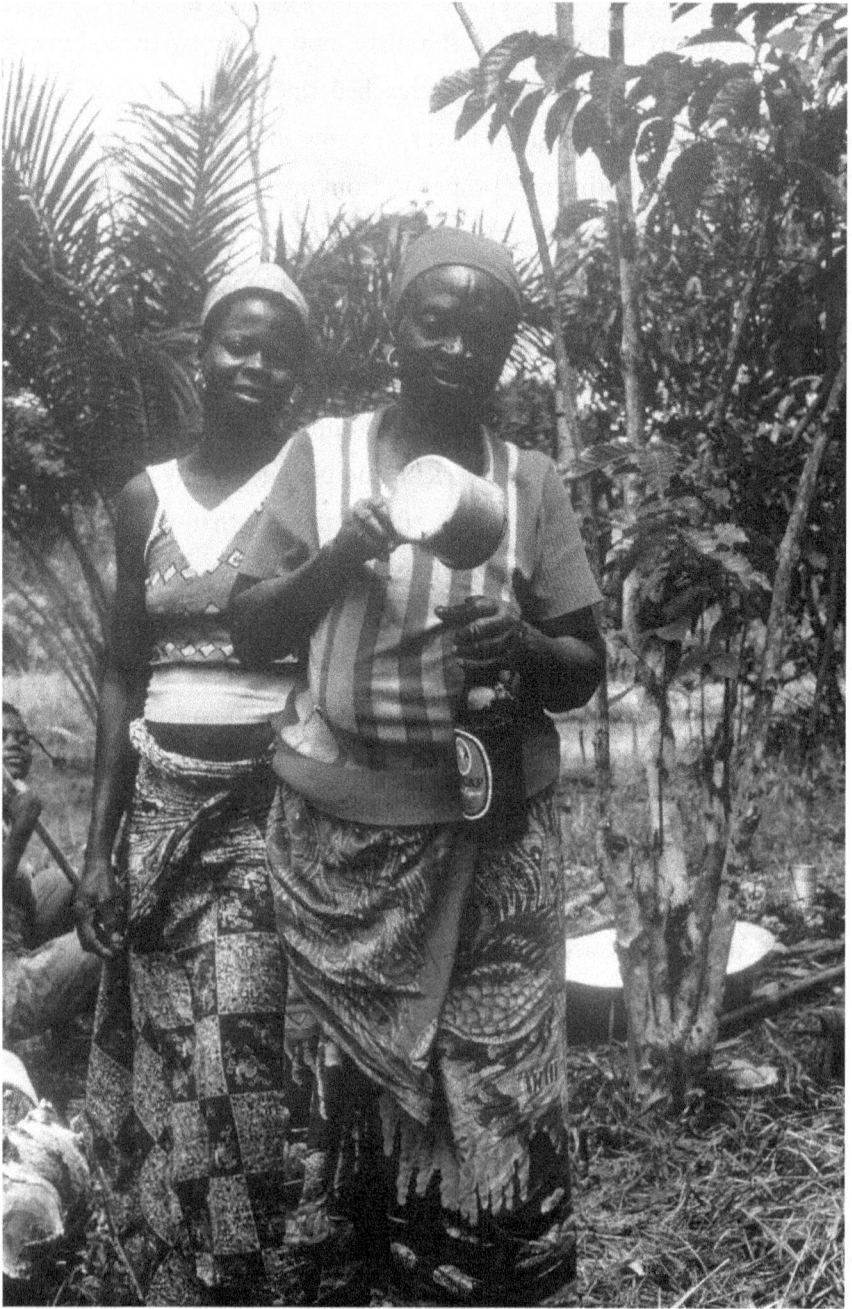

Bako and *Gozo* at pond side.

When people were sick here, the drums came out, and all did a circle dance around a fire giving the light to take away darkness, and around drums beating away the blocks that limit the light in life. Dancing away sickness. Sharing life energy by laying on hands to heal. Singing, touching, dancing the magical medicinal mandala-circle dance of life.

I lay at night on my back on my *paillote* floor, head to the center like a spoke of a wheel. All the roof poles above radiated out and down from the center like rays of the sun. The roof, the wheel, the sun, earth, universe started spinning. The great moving mandala of life focusing its infinite immensity to a point infinitely small in the center of my being. And the whole universe was within me and radiated from me.

Why Africa? To learn how other people live together on earth. To learn to live simply. To simply live, and to carry out the purpose of all people everywhere on earth. To give and share the love and light of our beings. From the Appalachian woods to African savanna. Being guided along the path by the light of life. And each different place, different people like prisms dividing the one light into their own colors reflecting their own beauty, complementing each color like a universal rainbow. And the root of universal is us. The universe begins with us. We create it. We are it. Let's live it in love.

EIGHT

The Empire Strikes Out–Impressions
Written at the Time of the Fall of Bokassa

1978

Another African dictator down, people wild in the streets, dancing, looting Bokassa's businesses, pillaging his palaces, defacing his photos, toppling his statues. The statues are being replaced by statues commemorating the students killed by the deposed emperor. New statues to serve as a reminder to remember Ngaragba, the prison, the massacre of the students, now martyrs, the 14 years of imperialism.

But how awakened have the people become, how aware? Is the consciousness changing in Africa? It must to create the situational changes. But how deep does it go? People have grown up with tribalism, colonialism, and imperialism. The people of Central Africa have been slaves to Bokassa. All the wealth went to him. All the international aid went to graft. High government officials with big bellies and big cars followed the example of their leader. People trained in France to emulate the French lifestyle, to amass personal fortunes at the expense of the masses. And it's easy to get away with it here. The population was spread out, isolated from the capital with no political consciousness and no communication except the royal

50

radio of empty rhetoric and imperial decrees declaring the latest means to squeeze the last *pata* from the people.

Even the people in the bush sought to emulate their ingrained example to look for someone to take advantage of. A power-tripping pyramid from the government to the bush. Where women were workers for their men, children were gofers who took out their frustrations by stoning dogs and chickens. Each tribe considered the other savage, and Pygmies were considered no more than animals.

The country had been on a 14 year decline. The infrastructure-roads, hospitals, and schools–deteriorated while the imperial palaces prospered. Teachers, doctors and officials rarely got paid–as most of the money and materials went to Bokassa.

But the people had accepted this or adapted to it. When there were no doctors or medicine, they turned to traditional treatments. And when roads completely deteriorated so no trucks can get through to buy cash crops–coffee, cotton, and tobacco–the people returned to self-sufficient farming and gathering.

Finally the lethal level of acceptance was reached. The students, the ones who became aware of their talents, couldn't suppress their feelings any longer. They took to civil disobedience to demonstrate their desires, to get what they themselves and their country deserved. As Bokassa demonstrated his dementia to the world, the students' blood flowed through the heart of Central Africa.

It took outright killings to produce action. After the massacre of 18 April 1979, international aid was cut, and several government officials left to protest Bokassa's tyranny. They went to France to establish a government in exile. This made Bokassa nervous, so he went to Libya to ask for arms and aid. Gaddafi said sure–they wanted a military base there to enhance their interests in Chad and other African countries. But even they didn't want Bokassa. While Bokassa was in Libya, the Libyans, behind Bokassa's back were planning a coup d'état to install Ange Félix Pattassé, a former Central African prime minister, as President and establish a puppet state.

But France was warned by a phone call from the incumbent prime minister Henri Maïdou. The French got there first with paratroopers. They installed David Dacko as a figurehead president under the guise of restoring democracy. Dacko, Bokassa's cousin, was president before Bokassa removed him by a coup 14 years ago. The French figured it would make good press to reinstall the "Dacko democracy." It appeared to be a French planned and executed coup, and the country is now basically a French colony, or "protectorate."

But if France weren't here, what would have happened? The country would be open to Libya, chaos, and a probable tribal war to wipe out Bokassa's tribe.

But why did France support Bokassa for so long? Why did they foot the bills for his foolishness, his coronation? The coronation, with columns, white horses, gilded carriages, and gold throne, cost over thirty million dollars, the annual national budget. Why did they bail out the budget when Bokassa kept the money for himself? And why didn't France hold Bokassa—a French citizen—for trial? Perhaps they'd be a bit embarrassed if the world knew of the price paid for an African playground.

Had the consciousness changed in Africa? What were Africans' limits of acceptance? Will they stop accepting and start to conscientiously re-create their continent? A year-long public trial of Bokassa ensued, with stories of cannibalism, crocodile and lion pits, and diplomatic dinners at his palace—serving diplomats for dinner!

For myself, I'd left my home in Boganangone to live among the animals in the Manovo-Gounda Saint Floris game park to do an ecological survey of the area. The park is in the farthest reaches of the middle of nowhere. Another American man, Bruce Hurlburg, and I were among the few human inhabitants with the exception of Chadian and Sudanese elephant poachers, illegal cattle herders, and fisherman. Also a French couple charged with park management and animal protection were there with their workers and eco-guards. We will concentrate on vegetation surveys, larger mammal habits, especially elephants, aerial surveys, and a bit of birding on the side.

Duti Nzoni, Cheshire.
Rest well, Cheshire

NINE

Manovo-Gounda Saint Floris
National Park

1978

"**S**ure, Bruce, sure this is the road–it's just where elephants strolled side by side holding trunks." We were the first vehicle in the game parks this year and were breaking the virgin path through the ten foot-high rainy-season grasses that have made the dirt track indistinguishable from the green-brown ocean. We considered doing our vegetation survey simply by identifying the grass seeds carpeting the truck-cab floor and spearing us as we drove. And we soon encountered the first and most ferocious animal species in the park–the terrible tsetse fly.

We had a specially adapted brush-breaking bar and a radiator screen mounted on the front of our Toyota Land Cruiser, and Moussa, our African *pisteur*, pathfinder, was perched on the hood conducting, orchestrating with hand signals, our way through the grass. Finally, we arrived at the first base camp on the Koumbala River.

We moved into a cement *paillote* with a grass roof about ten feet away from the river. Our office was on the *paillote* porch; our music, birds and river. Whenever the frustration of keying out grasses became too great, we would simply wade into the water neck deep and let it all flow away. At night we enjoyed a bioluminescent firefly show and a lion serenade. Each morning there was a fresh set of tracks through camp.

Office with a view.

By day we took drives to look for animals. Either Bruce or I drove with Moussa to guide, with the other one sitting on the truck roof to see above the grass. When the one on top saw something interesting, he thumped his foot on the roof like the Walt Disney *Bambi* rabbit Thumper, and we stopped for a look. Within the first two weeks we observed 18 previously unrecorded bird species for the area.

Seeing above the grass.

Our work as wildlife biologists combined reconnaissance walks and drives as well as systematic "road-strip censuses." We did these systematic census drives twice per year, at the same time each year. One person would drive the Toyota Land Cruiser, at no more than 25 kilometers per hour, and the other would sit on the roof with binoculars in hand, counting all the animals, including age and sex, and recording the data on a mini tape recorder. By doing these surveys at the same time, in the same place, we were able to begin to discern trends in the populations of key species. We also did aerial surveys of the park, flying a grid system of straight-line flights, traversing all the various habitats of the park. There was always a pilot (of course) and a navigator, and Bruce and I were observers, sitting in the backseat with our eyes fixed to the ground on either side of the plane. The plane flew at 300 feet at a constant speed, and a banner trailing back from the struts formed to band within which we counted all animals of all species. These surveys were also done at the same time each year so comparisons could be made. Later aerial surveys, here and throughout Africa, focused on live-elephant-to-carcass ratio to estimate the population declines due to poaching. Bleached bones are easy to see at 300 feet.

We assisted in carrying out a complete vegetation survey of the park, working with Bernard Peyre de Fabrègues of the Veterinary Institute in Paris, and cartographers helped to make the vegetation maps. We created a park herbarium and sent plants to various taxonomic experts around the world for identification.

In addition to the Land Cruiser, we also had a 175cc Yamaha motorcycle that I would use to ride elephant trails to map them out and to note where current elephant activity was. A *moto* was a great way of getting around, however, the tsetse flies saw the moving *moto*, and zeroed in on the blood on wheels. I had to wear jeans, a denim jacket, and gloves to keep the bugs from biting. The motion of the *moto* also excited the chase reaction of lions, and several times I had prides stalking me as I rode. I tied a compressed air horn on the handlebars, and when they began to converge, I'd sound the horn like a Mack truck. That tended to stall them enough for me to make tracks!

One morning, I took Bernard out on the *moto* to an inaccessible area of the park to collect plants. While we were out, I heard a group of elephants in a gallery forest, and I wanted to know what they were feeding on. Around midday, I took Bernard back to Koumbala for lunch, then I went back alone to check out the elephants. I went as far as possible on the elephant trail leading to the forest, then left the bike at the bottom of a hill, entered the forest, and found a perch to observe the elephants. I was so engrossed in elephant watching and note taking that I did not pay attention

Lions.

to the time, until I looked up from the dark gallery forest to see that the sun was setting. I did not want to be caught in the tall dry grass after dark, and needed to get to the other side of the river where the grass was burnt before nightfall. I got back to my bike, gave it a kick start, and headed back up the elephant trail through the tall grasses. As it was getting darker, I was going faster, jumping logs and rocks, playing Steve McQueen. Finally, I knew I would not make it to the river crossing in time, so I made a plan in my head to turn downhill around a bush 20 meters ahead, and find a way across the river wherever I hit it. Just as I was turning tight around the bush like a barrel chase, I looked down right into the golden glowing eyes of a lion two meters from me. His mane was dark and full, his body taut, ready to spring. My reaction was to stand up on the foot pegs, let go of the accelerator, wave my right hand and yell, in Sango, *"Mo gwe, Bamara!"*- (Lion, go away!) As my attention went to my near neighbor, I hit a clump of grass and stalled the motorcycle. I kept yelling and waving, while trying to kick-start the bike, now overheated with grass filling the flanges of the motor. I kicked, I yelled, and waved. He sat back a bit bewildered. It took five kicks of the *moto* before it started and I wheeled out of there leaving the lion to wonder what kind of antelope that was. Whiskey was in order when I got back to camp.

After a week of general survey in the Koumbala Camp area, we moved on to the second camp at the Gounda River Bridge. A few kilometers out we all but ran into a herd of 18 elephants, which came thundering and trumpeting out of the grass and across the road three meters in front of our truck. It takes a lot of grass to hide 18 elephants. A few more waterbuck and hartebeest and we arrived at the bridge camp.

Elephant in the grass.

As I sat by kerosene lamp light in again another *paillote* house, I could hear the trailing thunder, the last few drops of rain off the trees nestling into the grass of our roof, a lion roaring not far off, and the evening chatter of the few people living in this little outpost village. The rest of the world came close yet in some ways seems so distant. I read *Newsweek*, about another nuclear "accident" and the Pope's messages. No one is ever too distant from nuclear nonsense. How many mutants will it take till we know that too many Nuclear Regularity Commission officials have lied? The answer, my friend, is blowing in the radioactive wind.

The Pope called for world peace and unity through love. He called for simplification of our lifestyles. He called for a more equal sharing of the wealth, spiritual and material. But how can he achieve equality and unity when he continues the Catholic caste system of spiritual sexism? He called for the fraternity of men, but what about women? When are women going to be considered as more than silent background birthers, feeders, and workers for a male society? Why are women seen as spiritless beings in his revelations, restricted from their rightful priestly places? And somehow a distinction is still drawn between the marriage of two people and of all people through universal love. When will it be that people tune into their own spirit guides to lead them through life and not depend on divine delusions? He says politics are made by man, not God. Maybe that's true, but it's about time to put some godliness into politics. Gandhi said he who sees religion as separate from politics doesn't understand religion. Religion is living. Living is loving.

As Thoreau said, "Let us settle ourselves, and work and wedge our feet downward through the mud and slush of opinion, and prejudice, and tradition, and delusion, and appearance, that alluvion which covers the globe through Paris and London, through New York and Boston and Concord [and Cheshire], through church and state, through poetry and philosophy and religion, till we come to a hard bottom and rocks in place, which we can call reality, and say, This is, and no mistake; and then begin, having a *point d'appui*, below freshet and frost and fire, a place where you might find a wall or a state, or set a lamp-post safely, or perhaps a gauge, not a Nilometer, but a Realometer, that future ages might know how deep a freshet of shams and appearances had gathered from time to time."

In conversations with my park partner Bruce, he asked me how I would define my spiritual feelings. At first I said simply a Naturalist. And while watching red-throated bee-eaters swoop a rainbow arch into their nest colonies, while walking in the sun seeing the animals around us here, it came to me to describe myself as Bio-Theologist. Living is my religion. Biology, the study of life, is not just a job; it's a devotion to experiencing the Way of Life. Each bird sings a note in the song of life; every wave of wind in the savanna grass is a brushstroke on the canvas of life.

And the work I do with my body, my hands is but a dance. Bruce and I planted our little garden today. We plant as much for the joy of sowing as reverence for the reaping. To realize that within each seed life simply awaits the sun, the rain. And for the seed in me, let it ripen in the sun as I twine the trails of the earth, as I drink from life's fountain. And let the fruit of my being be bountiful.

We went for a drive to see animals. With the grasses at their height, we drove by instinct as well as by eyesight. It's like driving old roads through back pastures back home, through goldenrods and sumacs, through fields that have retired from feeding people's bellies and now feed a person's spirit. The home of the goldfinch and sparrow, pheasant and rabbit. There's something about a place succeeding from farm to forest again. A biologist would call it plant succession. When the farmer fails and nature succeeds. No success like failure. When I walk through such a field beneath the locust and wild cherry, a place going from tame to wild, so goes my mind. The parched plowed furrows of my mind come out of production and go fallow to catch any wild seed to sink its roots and give its shade.

We drove slowly along these tracks. The grasses blowing in the breeze suddenly bend and disappear beneath the brush bar of the truck. And for a while I'm once again in the back lot of my family's farm back home. I'm ten years old and learning to drive on just such a road on our old Farmall Cub tractor, my father standing on the drawbar behind me as we bounce along being together under the guise of doing some chore, mending some fence. Oh, what seeds were sown in those days of father and son!

If only our little town of Cheshire could see the value of fallow fields and young forests for the development of minds and not for the development of half-acre plots. These half-acre plots and condominiums are the caskets and funeral plots for a country town. Fell more trees, lay more roads, raise more houses, import more people, raise more taxes, force more farmers to sell, and so the epitaph of Cheshire is written. I say let your ears be filled with the sounds of life, the morning birds, the breeze in the trees and not the screech of tires and incessant bark of neighborhood hounds. Let the morning sun sparkle over dew-covered weeds, watch the flowers open in the sun. What soothing effect has the glare of pavement for a waking soul? See the profit of simplicity, not simply profit. Start in our own home to cure the cancer killing America.

The bite of a tsetse fly broke my reverie, my legs were sprinkled with stamens, anthers, and awns, and with my automatic tsetse fly swat reaction I occasionally drove a grass head spikelet stuck in my shirt into my skin. Because of high grasses and dispersal due to abundant water not many animals were seen. An occasional group of hartebeest, waterbuck, roan, or kob. But the birding was exceptional. Since the ground above eye level was solid grass, we looked to the trees and sky. Huge Abyssinian ground hornbills flushed up occasionally; carmine and red-throated bee-eaters soared and dove for bugs. The call of an African fish eagle echoed across the flood-plain, its white beacon head seen across the way. Red bishops perched on

African fish eagle.

Abyssinian ground hornbill.

Carmine bee-eater.

a grass stem rode the wind or flew bumblebee-like from perch to perch. Doves cooed, hawks and vultures scoured the grasslands from above.

We stopped at salines–salt lick areas–ancient termite mounds in which mineral by-products were deposited. The animals congregate in those areas to dig and eat the salty soil. Again, because of rainy season dispersal these areas were not heavily frequented, but tracks told what had been around. Everything from rhino to roan to lion was represented. With Moussa's help we learned the tracks, their age and sex. Of the better samples we made plaster casts. We also made collections of grasses from each vegetation habitat to compile in a herbarium.

Our initial project was to determine the status of the western black rhino in the park. We choose a study area in the park's southern highlands and set up a camp on the Sakala River. This area was accessible only by foot and unexplored recently, but previously inhabited by people. We found evidence of early iron forges and caves complete with paintings depicting

Moussa with cave paintings.

people spearing elephants from the cliff walls. These caves had never been recorded previously.

And when I share my dreams, my plans for my life with others, trails to walk, mountains to climb, rivers to canoe, people to know, gardens to hoe, it may be future tripping, but all voyages begin with a dream.

Bruce and Richard at field camp.

I sometimes see a spark in their eyes. It glows, and then darkens, and sometimes they say, "I'd like to live like that, but I don't have the time"–careers, schools, jobs. I see people so caught up in making a living they forget about living. I say to all, dream on! Don't stifle your daydreams because they're not a "productive" use of your time. We're not machines droning on, taking only time to refuel. Dream on and live your dream! A dream born from the pureness of your inner being, energized by your soul's strength, carried out with faith in love and life creates your own reality and the expression of your true self.

Again a quote from Thoreau, "I went to the woods because I wished to live deliberately, to front only the essential facts of life and see if I could not learn what it had to teach, and not, when I came to die, discover that I had not lived."

Let life be your school, living your career.

2015

I went on to a doctorate at Yale and a career with World Wildlife Fund. I continued to live deliberately. While with Peace Corps, as a fisheries extension agent as well as in the park, I was observing birds and made a species list of about 700 species, their habitat associations and their status, earning a master's degree. I sound like a dreamer in these early writings, but I see that I was also an entrepreneur, energized by the life I loved, gaining credibility by tacking on a degree to what I wanted to do anyway, writing grants to the major conservation organizations, becoming known. When I completed my doctoral thesis on the feeding ecology of the lowland gorilla in southwestern CAR in 1990, WWF invited me to become a program officer in Washington, D.C., where I stayed until 2014 as vice president for the Africa and Madagascar Program.

So, school and career. But right livelihood. Orion, when young, always said that he wanted to do what Daddy does–to save the world. Then he developed a passion for music. He wanted to go to school for sound engineering. Some dads may have pushed for a MBA. But I developed a career from following gorillas in the forest. I said, "Follow your passion; just be good at it and make it work." He did. He's living deliberately.

TEN

Bring Your 'Binocs' to Breakfast

1978

"Bring your 'binocs' to breakfast" was the theme at Camp Gounda as the sun rose over the floodplains and the birds came to life. Scarlet-chested sunbirds were already busy in the lavender *Anogeissus* flowers and long-tailed beautiful sunbirds in the white puff *Syzgyium* blossoms.

"Oatmeal again–but look over the floodplains–yellow-billed egrets following a buffalo herd and above a Verreaux's eagle and marabou storks circle in, and there's something new and different–a white-winged black tern dipping along the river."

"Pass the honey, please–shhhh–over there-a pair of kob."

Not a moment's peace with the chatter of a black-headed weaver colony, their woven nests hanging over the river. So much to look at. A pair of black-breasted barbets, their heavy white bills beamed in the sun. Several Sacred ibis painted bright white on green as they arched down into the river, their long contrasting black necks and bill outstretched.

Camp Gounda is a pleasant little place along the Gounda River in the Manovo-Gounda Saint Floris National Park. The park consists of

4.7 million acres in the north eastern watershed of the Central African Republic where another Peace Corps volunteer, Bruce, and I were doing an ecological survey of the area.

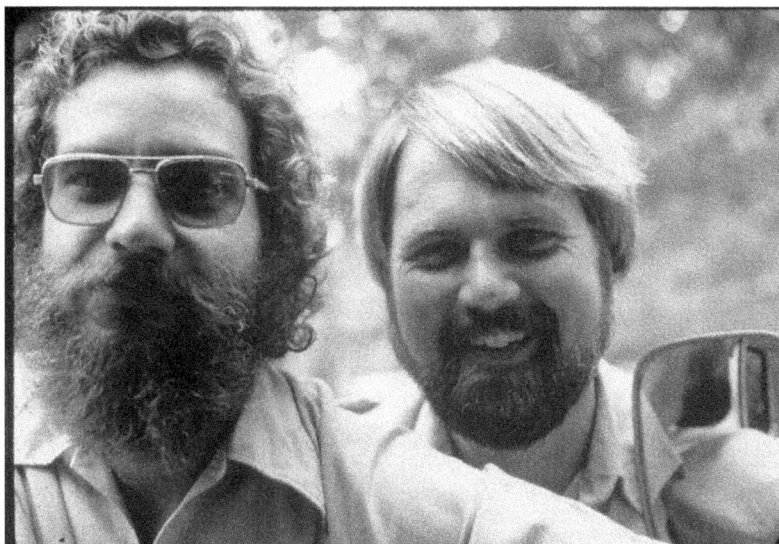

Richard and Bruce.

The camp was made for tourists, but it was just Bruce, myself, and the dozen or so Africans who work here. The camp consisted of several round cement *paillotes* with grass over corrugated metal roofs. Each was divided into three rooms with two beds and a sink with running water flowing from a water pumped from the river. There were also showers and toilets fed from the water tower. The *paillotes* are white-washed, and beside the door of each room on the outside wall was painted an animal found in the park. The room Bruce and I used there was *tchon-d'jo*, African hunting dog. There was a kitchen with a wood burning oven and an open-air grass-roofed *paillote* for eating under. Several pirogues around the camp are used as planters. The African workers, according to the French fashion, lived in their separate village behind the camp.

After our *petit dejeuner*, we packed up the truck, push started it (dead battery), and headed north. We crossed the Gounda River, the kob and waterbuck watching us pass. A fish eagle served as sentry over the crossing. We emerged on the road which was well worn though no cars have passed in weeks. Elephant tracks have erased all others, and in passing they had greatly enriched the soil of the road with their droppings.

We rolled on through dry low woodland. Little ourebi antelope dodged behind termite mounds, then in a blast of dry heat and sunshine, we emerged on the great Dongolo floodplains. With the exception of a few clumps and wooded termite mounds, this area is flat open grassland, under a foot of water and eight feet of grass in the rainy season. Now it was dry and burned over. Waterbuck, kob, topi, hartebeest, and buffalo dotted the plains.

Here as everywhere the animals were well adapted to their environment. Ostrich with long necks and legs gazed above the grass and paced across the plains. Secretary birds in their plumed bonnets searched for snakes. Their long scaly yellow legs defy any fangs; their strong talons and beak kill quickly. Giraffes glided gracefully through the grass, their long necks allowing them to browse the high branches for fresh leaves.

In the Dongolo Mare (a waterhole separated from the river in the dry season), we watched a waterfowl fishing frenzy. White and pink-backed pelicans paddle, pouches filled with fish. Monstrous marabou storks marauded the mare, throat sacs sagging with *soussou*. Spoonbills and openbills searched the shallows. Wood ibis and saddle-billed storks seized their share with scissor-like motion. Hadada, glossy, and sacred ibis probed for fish with long, curved bills. Great white, black-headed, and grey heron stalked

Secretary bird.

Ostrich.

the reeds with the well-hidden bitterns. Hammerkops hawked amid the hummocks, pied kingfishers hovered and dove, all finding their fill of fish. Pintail and fulvous tree ducks filtered for food. Plovers, sandpipers and stilts, stalked along the sandbars. Fish eagles were perched to plunge. Terns and swallows skimmed the surface. Yellow-billed and little egrets hung out on hippos' backs while yellow-billed oxpeckers picked their ticks.

Wood storks fishing.

A lion hunted a hartebeest and ate it in a *Tamarindus*-shaded termite mound next to the mare. Five species of vultures took their share while black kites dove for morsels. On through the plains, a shy reedbuck tried to hide in the grass. Pale and Montagu's harriers hunted low over the plains. We made camp at Vakaga River crossing, had lunch, and moved on north to Gata Mare.

Saddle-bill storks.

At the mare 1,300 hippos hung out lazily lounging in the shallow murk, sleeping with the head of one on the back of another. If one rolled over it created a ruckus and roar from the rest, otherwise pink-mouthed toothy yawns and occasional grunts was the extent of the action. Actually, the yawns and grunts are a complex language signifying the hierarchy within the herd.

Back to the Vakaga again for the night, and oh, what a night it was! A *soir sauvage*—wild night. We went to "bed" to the normal sounds, the whistle of kob, the song of the frogs. "Bed" meant a grass mat on the ground, with a mosquito net strung between four fishing spears stuck into the ground. Sleep came easy, but it didn't last long. My dreams were disturbed by the howl of hyenas passing on the road by our camp. Just as I drifted off again the trumpet of an elephant

Hippo yawn.

Mare Gata.

nearby sent me through my mosquito net. The elephants were out for an evening stroll along the river when, lo and behold: humans. I had to get up and direct traffic around our camp. It took 15 minutes for them to pass single file.

So much for sleep. Soon we had a lion chorus. Two on our side of the river just outside our camp, one on the other side, and two more farther off. We kept the fire blazing. With the fire the lions kept their distance, but the African hunting dogs wandered right on in barking and carrying on. Then a group of hippos moved into the river, grunting and splashing like they owned the place, which of course they do, so I just enjoyed the hippo harmony, the stars, and the sunrise.

We returned to Camp Gounda, and some French tourists had brought us a new battery and some mail. News from family and the latest discussion between the Cheshire taxpayers and the school board.

African hunting dog-*tchon d'jo.*

It's time for the people of Cheshire and the world find a piece of solid ground outside the shaky systems of spiraling growth and development, to sit back and see what's happening. I apply my Bio-Theologist viewpoint to Connecticut just as I do here in the park. I look at the succession of ecological-people-illogical events happening in the Cheshire biosphere. Just as declining rains can stimulate the succession of a swamp to woodland, rapidly rising taxes turn our country town into an overcrowded metropolis. As taxes rise, farmers and landowners are forced to sell out to developers, trees are plowed under, fields are paved over, and-the white aluminum signs are nailed on. Then all the nice new families move in on their half-acre plot with their kids and dogs. Then of course they want schools and sidewalks, snow-shoveling service from the town, and taxes rise again. Half-acre lots are the funeral plots for a country town.

Since 80 percent of the education costs comes from land taxes, farmers or just someone with a fallow field in which to watch the flowers grow, regardless of whether they have children in the schools or not, are forced to foot the school bills for a half-acre family of five.

It's time the taxpayers turn the tide of this tempest. Limits to growth must be set. Our tax system continually contributes to the quantity of those to be educated and not to the quality of education. The education tax dollars must not be spent simply to provide space for increasing enrollment as opposed to providing the maximum means for the personal development of the individuals to be educated. People need open space as well as classroom space to learn about themselves. We can't continue to pave over nature's own classrooms and install temporary classrooms in our school parking lots.

In 1980 any system, that encourages population growth and the permanent loss of our open land is contrary to the laws of nature and will lead to the deterioration of the quality of life.

In the past, people who stated, "I'm a taxpaying citizen" implied that they were responsible ones. Now those who pride themselves as being responsible community members must work to change an irresponsible unbalanced system and put their conscious efforts into re-creating a living system stressing the development of personal potential in balance with the natural world we are a part of.

Why not an educational tax system that taxes a family for the number of family members using the school system? This would encourage family size limitation and encourage open space preservation.

The lessons of life come from both inside and outside the classroom. Botany classes become meaningless when the wildflowers are gone. Music means more if you've heard the wind in a hemlock forest. Interpersonal relationships become clearer when you are aware of your relationship with nature.

We humans are unlike the hippos I saw at Gata Mare. We cannot continue to subsist asleep simply supporting our weight in our rising sewage. Soon we may drown in it.

2015

You may say I was a dreamer, à la John Lennon. The farms of Cheshire have all grown MacMansions. A paradigm shift. When I was in high school, my grandmother was 90. I would sit with her for hours and she told me stories of New Haven when she was a young girl: horse races on Whalley Avenue, the blacksmith shop where a highway entrance ramp is now, gathering blackberries where the Magic Mile Shopping Mall stands now. We don't remember what life was like, what the world was like, except through the stories of those who remember when. It is what it is, but what comes next for a world full of people?

ELEVEN

Breakdown

1978

Back your way there may be a slight problem with rabbits and woodchucks in your garden, but what does one do to keep the elephants from eating your eggplants and trampling your turnips? Just a minor problem of living in an African wildlife park. But the pleasures surely outweighed any possible problems, to have seen a place on earth so completely natural, purely pristine. Where a lioness stalking a waterbuck will crouch directly in front of our open Land Cruiser without flinching, without breaking the bond of concentration connecting her and her intended meal. When a cinnamon-maned male barely blinked to acknowledge our approach within ten meters. Where my heart pounded in my chest as we slowly, silently slipped within 30 meters of an elephant herd. Where galloping giraffe glided with god-like grace across the plains like waves of wind in the grass.

From where I sat in the shade of a *paillote* on a curve of the Gounda River I could hear the splash of a Nile perch in the water, the calls of lily-trotters amongst the weeds. The blaze of blue of the wings of a gray-headed kingfisher streaked across the green of grass. Scarlet-breasted sunbirds sipped at the fountain of flowers planted in a pirogue to brighten the camp.

Across the plain. kob antelope grazed in the green. Red-throated bee-eaters darted and danced in their six-colored suits with brilliant blue tails. The white head of an African fish eagle beamed brightly among the branches. Its slicing shrill stopped the more subtle sound of birds and wind. Huge Cape buffalo grazed half-hidden by high savanna grass accompanied by red-billed oxpeckers along for a free ride and meal. When approached they bound and bounce, stomp and stamp, doing a water buffalo waltz. Carmine bee-eaters constructed crowded crimson colonies in the riverbanks. Topi and hartebeest did their long-faced comedy act. There were fleeting flashes of roan antelope and we caught distant glimpses of giant eland. Striped bushbuck struck a frozen stance atop a termite mound merging their colors with the streaking sunlight and red earth. Red-flanked duikers darted directly into the denseness. Hundreds of hippos hung out during the heat of the day in the green water.

Buffalo.

"It must be a lion kill," I said to my partner Joel. Joel was a Peace Corps Volunteer building a bridge in the park. Our Land Rover had broken down, and we were walking the five or six kilometers back to camp.

Black kites and vultures dipped into the grass thirty meters ahead and lighted in the trees. That and the absence of antelope caused us to stop short, alert to the aura of lion. I cupped my ears to listen–only the whoosh of wings and screech of the scavengers. We moved on, cautiously climbing trees to survey the scene. Splattered blood on matted grass told us our instincts were correct. We moved on, eyeing every climbable tree as an escape route. Behind every bush we imagined *bamara*. The meters were like miles. Every branch of dry leaves was a lion lurking. Then to the left and behind on the periphery of vision, where imagination plays its greatest tricks, a glimpse of a shape matching in color but not in form with trunks of trees and leaves of grass. The reality rose distinct with slightly arched shoulders, slightly lowered head, slightly tensed eyebrows, eyes catching and holding mine.

Damara.

I said with my eyes, "Just passing through, don't bother getting up." She replied, "We were just eating anyway." So on we went.

When we returned to tow the Land Rover back to camp, three well-fed lionesses and a lion lounged in the shade by the road.

So now we were left with an old Ford van to make the 140-kilometer trip back to the main base camp. We made it to within fifty-five kilometers when we sank to the axles in a swamp. So again we walked. We left the van at 5 P.M.; again each tree was a place to flee. We walked on. Just before complete darkness we froze, hearing noise in the bush ahead. We stood, ears and eyes alive. We found the sound not only ahead but all around us. Then ahead a massive gray movement slightly lighter than the darkened bush seeming like a cloud of fog. We realized we had walked right into the middle of an elephant herd. We were downwind of most and moved to the base of the biggest tree around to plan our strategy. We let out with whoops and wails and unbird-like bird sounds and were answered by crashing bush in all directions as the elephants scattered. We walked on.

And we walked on. Constant alertness, mounting fatigue. The sensation of falling asleep on my feet. Sitting to rest to gather strength, almost fatally falling asleep on the ground. We finally took to the trees for slightly safer sleep, balanced in the branches until the cold breeze and biting ants drove us on.

Finally a second wind and a second elephant encounter in the darkness before dawn. As we walked numbly along, our sounds and scent sparked a herd of over a hundred elephants into stampeding, crashing, trumpeting parallel to the path we were walking. Then they switched directions–to our direction. We stampeded to the nearest tree. We could have jumped on the back of an elephant as they passed beneath our perch. We stayed, gathering strength until the first light of dawn to go the last 15 kilometers to camp.

The sun rose, a many-colored morning sky. We were greeted by gentle giraffe grazing knee-deep in dew-glazed grass. We too drank the dew and descended into camp in time for breakfast.

Yes, it was humbling to live in a place on earth so natural. It was an honor to be a part of it, to share its life, light and darkness. It was a thrill to walk into the heart, depend on the same instincts as all its inhabitants from antelopes to eagles to us, all existing as one—where such contrivance as cars are out of their element and subject to the elements. We were able come back to our elemental instincts of life.

TWELVE

Saline Stakeout

1978

It was a Sunday morning sunrise saline stakeout. Bruce and I arrived at first light and got hidden among the laterite boulders in the middle to see what happens during a day at a natural salt lick area.

Saline stakeout.

Grunts and groans from the west and a herd of buffalo moved in to the edge, sniffed around, caught our scent, and then stomped off. We heard their grunts moving around to the east. The sunrise ignited the rocks and eroded earth into flaming red. A huge harrier hawk hung upside down on a dead tree feeding on insects beneath the loose bark. It seemed like a strange habit for such a large bird. I heard the distant roar and following grunts of a lion moving in from the west.

The rocks we were hiding in were practically undermined by elephants digging with their tusks for salt. It looked like a miner had been at work with a pickax exposing the red earth streaked with white salts. The area all around was eroded by animal activity, and the tracks of all the myriad beings inhabiting the area were represented.

Elephants.

Every time I moved my head or shoulders I was deafened by the buzz of tsetse flies hanging out on my back, piercing a denim jacket and

T-shirt, and there was no mistaking their bite. It was swat first, look later. And seldom was a single swat sufficient. Everyone develops his or her own tsetse technique. Mine was swat, roll, pop. A swat will stun and crumple, but rarely kill. They're like those trick birthday candles that can't be blown out–a spark keeps bursting back to flame, and they bite again.

The sun had gone from red to gold, and we heard the buffalo arching off towards the floodplains to pass the day grazing. I readjusted my body to get a bit of blood back to my legs–if the tsetse has left enough to complete circulation. I don't think it was cramps from squatting between the boulders that made my feet go to sleep-it was blood loss from tsetse bites. So that's the sleeping sickness tsetse causes!

A long-tailed yellow-breasted pygmy sunbird sipped the succulent flowers, while a dark chanting goshawk stood surveying the saline on a dead branch. The high-pitched whistle of gray hornbills heralded the rising sun. Three stone partridges paraded through the parched grass below me. A flock of twenty or thirty brown parrots fed in the hardened mud; their bright blue-green underparts flashed like a firefly when they flew. The roaring rush of wings of hundreds of ring-necked doves applauded the rising sun. The whole area was alive with chirping, squawking, whistling, barking, and singing as life awakened to the dawn.

I noticed a big baboon high in a tree at the southwestern edge of the saline. He sat on a branch with his forearms on his knees surveying the situation, apparently a sentry for the troops behind. Soon his buddies showed up barking and bouncing, making threatening gestures towards us. They made short, abrupt jumps, shake branches, knock bark off trees, bark, scratch, and showed their colossal canines.

The lizards had warmed sufficiently to scamper about. A brown-backed turquoise-headed agama did pushups on a rock near me.

As the sun began to warm, the mixture of bird songs funneled down into throaty dove calls, and carmine and red-throated bee-eaters reflected rainbow colors as they flew.

Off came my shirt so I too could reflect and absorb some sun colors, and on went my grass and leather pointed wizard hat given to me by the Mbororo chief in Boganangone before I left there. The Mbororo (Fulani) are nomadic Muslim cattle herders, and this hat is faded from many long days following his cattle in the savanna sun.

Even though cattle were a way of life for a lot of people here and elsewhere, I see little sense in them. In this country they were a major cause of the decline of wildlife, as cattle herds had displaced natural mammal populations. The Mbororo have poisoned off the predators—lions, leopards—to protect their stock. With cattle come diseases—filaria from flies, and parasites from impure meat. When herd size exceeded grazing capacity, desertification followed in the drier northern areas. At least the cattle here were grass fed. In the U.S. ninety percent of all grains produced are used to feed cattle. Talk about sacred cows! Americans worship their sacred steaks! Look at the human sacrifices made to them. Cereals that could feed people are pumped into cattle. How many pounds of grain and acres of land went into that McDonald's quarter pounder? How much life energy is funneled down into cows, then further into humans—and how much is lost along the way! Consider the heart disease caused by the buildup of indigestible animal fat in the arteries of Americans. We could feed the world on one half the land used to feed American cattle and produce a healthier population.

Zebu.

I say again, simplify and enrich! Let life and light be shared by all earthly beings and not reduce it all to human life. Cut out a level in the food chain, and link yourself closer to the earth. All food is simply packaged light, and the closer it is to the sun the purer it is. We must learn globally to limit human population growth and adopt a more ecologically sound lifestyle. In a world of modern inefficiency, we must become more efficient feeders. Let us tread more softly and be fed more lightly.

Meanwhile, back at the saline, a pair of giant eland moved in from the east. It looks like white paint dripped down their striped sides; their long, gracefully twisted horns reflect the sun. Their smaller cousin the bushbuck blended in with the red and white earth. A warthog scared an ourebi—it did fully extended ballerina bound across the baked earth. Her gracefulness contrasted with the stout directness of the warthog, which looks a bit bizarre with its big tusks and tail standing straight up like a periscope.

Giant eland.

A red-cheeked cordon bleu posed two meters from me. A green-bodied, red-winged, white-crested turaco flashed across the clearing. Two European hoopoes landed in a tree, and a bateleur eagle circled overhead and with its short tail and seemed to be flying backwards.

As the sun lowered, we unbent our knees and put down our binoculars and headed back to camp. A swim in the river, and meditation by the rapids was in order, then dinner. Tonight our friend and cook Jean prepared the old standard and my favorite–*riz-ngunza*-rice and manioc-leaf sauce.

The sky darkened quickly, the new moon was moving toward its first quarter. Venus hung over the horizon. A buffalo snorted as it moved inland for the night and a lion began its night song. I looked around the darkened horizon, as the glow of grass fires set by poachers penetrates the night. The poachers burned the grass to become more efficient killers. They were mostly Chadian and Sudanese horsemen. Each dry season, they moved south with their herds and kill elephants on horse-back with spears. Formerly, they took slaves, and more recently, they also killed giraffes for their tails, which are used in Arab weddings; rhinos were killed for their horns, a false aphrodisiac to enhance some man's ego and for dagger handles; pythons, crocodiles, and leopards for skins to sell; antelope for meat; and fish to dry and sell.

With spear alone, in one dry season, we estimated that they killed ten percent of the 2,000-strong elephant herd. In the early 1980's the spears were replaced by automatic weapons, and whole herds fell. During the wars in Sudan, these horsemen became the Janjaweed, and terrorized the Darfur region just north of the border with CAR. Now, as part of the army of North Sudan, these international terrorists, having wiped out all of northern CAR's elephants, must go further afield, killing up to 650 elephants in Cameroon's Bouba NJida National Park, and trying to get to the last elephant stronghold, deep in the equatorial forests.

Poached elephant carcasses.

Leopards and crocodiles were seldom seen. Elephants were on the decline and were changing their habits due to poaching pressure. For every ivory necklace worn, let the wearer feel the weight of the entire elephant around his neck; every ivory ornament is inscribed with the blood of these beautiful beings lying butchered in the sun, all these beautiful beings being reduced for human profit and vanity.

It was Thanksgiving and I expressed my gratitude for the life I love. This Thanksgiving I showed my gratitude for the light that had sustained me for another year by taking less and giving more. This Thanksgiving I killed no bird, broke no bread, but instead gave the unnecessarily over-taxed earth a day off from feeding me. This year I fasted for Thanksgiving and meditated on giving light and love to help sustain the other earthly beings. This Thanksgiving I called on all people to take–or give–at least one day per month for fasting, purifying, and contemplating your position in the universe and to spend the rest of your days re-creating and rejoicing in its glory. Love, purify, glorify, and remember that we share the light of life with the other miraculous myriad creatures.

2015

Reading over these notes, I recall another "saline stakeout." Jean-Luc Temporal, the French park manager and I were scouting out the *falaise* or cliff face, where the southern highlands stepped down to the northern plains. The western black rhinos tended to follow the contours below the hills as *Gardinia sp.* and other favored plant species grew in this habitat. Rhinos are as blind as a bat and follow the same paths, kicking their droppings into middens. By kicking their manure, they tracked their scent on their feet and left a scent trail to follow. On my motorcycle, we found rhino tracks and began to follow them. They crossed the Gounda Bridge road and continued south. We followed them into a saline, and there, in a wallow, a gray rhino lay blending well with the gray mud. Jean-Luc and I climbed separate trees with a view of the rhino. In the heat, the black-fly-like sweat bees swarmed around our eyes. We waited. The rhino surged, then settled back into the mud. Hours went by, the tree branch dug into my leg. But the rhino hadn't moved for at least an hour. I climbed down and poked it with a very long stick, ready to fly back up to my perch. It didn't move. The last surge was its last breath.

We came back the next day with a truck, pulled it out of the wallow, and discovered the gunshot wound in its flank. It went into the mud to try to ease its pain.

The Gounda Bridge road was a national road, and colorful commercial vehicles, painted in bright colors with sayings from the Koran, traveled between CAR and Sudan with goods and contraband. The rhino likely crossed the road as a vehicle approached, and the driver took a potshot at a valuable quarry.

My first project in the parks was determining the status of western black rhinos. Minus one. We estimated 30 left in this park the size of the state of Connecticut. The sub species is now extinct. Will elephants be gone by the turn of this century?

THIRTEEN

Dry North to Dense Forest South

1978

Since I last wrote to you all, I went from Africa to America and back. I traveled by plane and train, Pygmy path and pirogue. I spoke many languages, to many people. I spoke to flowers and friends. I listened to the language of life. I heard the chainsaws roar in Maine, I saw the ancient African forests fall before the bulldozer blade. I listened to people's plans for wider, faster roads; I saw their developments dig deeper, destroying more. They tried to keep on going, desperately dreaming the American dream of progress and prosperity no matter what. Hanging on to the hope that they could have it all, ecologically, socially and politically, they rallied behind Ronald Reagan. We all want it all till nothing is left. We can only have it all if we leave it all alone. It seems that the earth will have to heal herself in spite of her human inhabitants. Those that open their hearts to help this healing are those that will inherit the earth.

I joined you from the northern provinces of Cameroon, where my park partner Bruce and I were visiting the Garoua Wildlife School. This school serves French-speaking West Africa as a training center for African wildlife technicians. Four Central African students were studying here, hoping that they would become counterparts in our Central African wildlife programs. The school was very well organized and staffed, with an excellent herbarium and library.

In my four years in Central African Republic, this was my first time to circulate in another African country. Cameroon was generally 10 to 20 years ahead of Central Africa in development but still retained some far-out traditional cultures. Up north the Fulani women were bedecked in brilliant fabrics with kilos of silver and brass braided in their hair, bangles and bracelets on their ears, arms, and ankles, rings in their noses, fantastically tattooed faces, balancing great gourds of milk on their heads. Men also had feathers and beads braided in their hair and were wearing long, loose colorful robes.

Fulani women in northern Cameroon.

Fulani women.

Garoua was a town of mosques, with Muslims chanting their prayers five times a day sometimes in the streets touching their foreheads to the sidewalks. It was a town of contrasts–the Mbororo in their traditional splendor were hailing a taxi to take them back to their villages and cattle. The Benué River flows past a backdrop of desert–mountains and pastel plateaus. People fished with large wood-framed dip nets about ten feet in diameter raised and lowered into the river by a lever-like hinged handle underneath a modern half-kilometer long bridge leading into town. A tiny donkey was being led across the bridge with a bicycle strapped to its back.

The whole north was served by paved roads and "bush taxis,"-vans in which about 45 people are packed to the max on minimally padded seats, and they were never full–they always insisted on fitting a few more paying passengers in.

There were hotels in all the major towns ranging from the Ritz to the pits. People were generally friendly to indifferent to whites; a minimum of patronizing or favoritism and no people were holding up their babies to see the *munju's* and no children chanting "Munju!, Munju!" at every stop as in Central Africa. Tourists were tolerated, no longer a rarity, and were barely noticed as folks go about their life.

We packed our backpacks to leave Garoua and stood in the shade of a huge baobab tree, hanging heavy with fruit, to hitch a ride on the paved road north. Soon a car stopped, we haggled over road fare, and were off through the surrounding Sahelian savanna circled by arid mountains like those found in Arizona, shrouded in Harmattan haze. Between the large towns were small villages of round mud brick, or grass houses with thatched roofs grown over with gourd and squash vines. Each little family village was surrounded by woven grass or mud walls. Tall millet with ripe brown heads bent in the breeze, while long horned zebu cattle, sheep, and goats grazed, tended by boys with clean-shaven heads.

We stopped at the market town of Billibe with a mélange of sounds–sheep baying, Muslim voices mixed with the myriad hues of flowing blue, white, yellow, and pink robes and embroidered prayer hats. We bought fresh bananas and guavas for the road and moved on. Small donkeys lazed in the shade, and azure blue Abyssinian rollers perched on acacia shrubs. The mountains grew high and ragged then expanded into flat harsh thorn bush country with dramatic rock outcroppings. Occasional ancient baobab trees–the symbol of Sahelian Africa, almost absent from Central Africa–stood as weathered witness to African history, bearing fruit for its future.

In a cloud of desert dust we rolled into Maroua. Already, during the very debut of the dry season, the two rivers that water the town disappeared underground and into the sky. The broad sandy riverbeds were pocked with pools where people dug small bathing holes, finding water six inches below the sand. The rivers had their beds on top while the water flows beneath.

We happened to hit town the day the presidents of Niger and Cameroon were meeting there, so the town was alive with people in from the country-side clad in their best traditional costumes dancing in the presidents' honor and to our pleasure. Later, I sat in a back alley bar, drank a Chadian Gala beer to wash away the Cameroonian dust, and a record player scratched out a French song while I wrote to you in English. A small world.

At the Fête de Présidents (celebration for the presidents), the streets were lined with hundreds of horsemen in full dress regalia—robes, and turbans, swords and spears, horses draped in colors, saddles worked with silver.

Maroua horseman.

From Maroua, we caught a bush taxi to backtrack to Ngoundere. The road wound precariously through the mountains, along the cliffs, and into the broad Benoue valley. Our bush taxi crawled along in first gear to avoid the shortcut over the cliffs into the valley far below. All forty of us scrunched, sardine-like, into the van breathed a sigh of relief as the last turn was negotiated and the breeze of faster motion cooled us off.

Ngoundere was a breezy town high on a plateau with the spires of the mosque towering over all and Fulani traders hawked their wares in the central market. In all these towns, small hole-in the wall "chop shops" sold rice and all had cold Coke, Pepsi, Fanta, and other sugar-filled delights imported from the Western world, as well as Cameroonian-brewed beer and soda.

In Ngoundere 500 cfa (Central African francs, +/- $2.00) got us a completely Westernized apartment at the American-Norwegian Lutheran Mission. Our apartment was in one of the 50 or so American-style ranch houses for missionaries who are "sacrificing their lives to save the savages." From some discussions with the missionaries I learned that they want nothing more than to completely change the African cultures. They felt that Muslim and Bantu beliefs were entirely invalid as they differ from what they *know* is the only truth. So they continue to bribe, pressure, and belittle the Africans into accepting their white God. What difference does it make how people visualize their spirituality? Whether Mohammed, Christ, Buddha, birds or trees-the same force of life and love flows through all, all paths like spokes of a wheel leading to the center.

From Ngoundere we booked passage on the Cameroonian Express Railway to Yaoundé, the capital city. The supposed 12-hour trip became 24 hours with breakdowns and banana buying along the way. Yaoundé was a very vital and growing city.

Another two muddy days through the southern forest in a bush taxi and I lay in the *soleil d'Afrique* (African sun), on the beach of Kribi, with the surf pounding behind. A whole new aspect of Africa for me: from the center to the edge–where Africa meets the Atlantic. The Lobé River *chutes* (waterfalls) mix the fresh water of the interior forests with the salt of the sea. Fisherman worked their nets and lines from pirogues at the mouth of the estuary. We set up camp beneath a palm, ate coconuts, mangos, and shrimp with beautiful Kribien beach people and perfected our body surfing. A magical place where the earthly elements merged and mystical powers flowed. On the rocks by the sea so many visions came to me.

> *You came like a dream from the mists*
> *Of the falls that plunge into the sea.*
> *Where the palms give their shade and*
> *The sun gives it warmth you gave yourself to me.*

> *You appeared like a Muse, we laughed like the wind.*
> *We ate coconuts by the sea.*
> *The love that we shared as full as the ocean*
> *You were sent by the gods, my Kribienne.*

> *The moon was so full it framed your face.*
> *The storm clouds raced all around the*
> *Thunder of the chutes, the rush of the waves,*
> *You child of the earth, my Kribienne.*

The tide fell back and you were gone,
I walk the widening sands.
Like the veil that hovers over the shimmering chutes,
You're between heavens and earth, my Kribienne.

We left Kribi with the waning of the moon and the receding tides. We re-entered the Central African Republic in the southwestern forest along the Sangha River. In the town of Nola we bought a pirogue and pushed off into the morning fog to float with the river into the depths of the forest. The deep gray of mist merged with the green of the foliage, the heavy hazy silence broken by the dripping dew and the ripple of the river on hanging roots.

Magical, misty forest.

We drifted and listened to life sounds that slice the silence and sightless fog. We heard the screeching of gray parrots as they streaked through the mist. The sudden chilling clamor of monkeys echoed between the forested river banks. Huge black and white casqued hornbills mooed and meowed. We saw occasional splash of a crocodile sliding off a muddy bank. Layered veils of colonial spider's webs hung silver in the gray. Hanging seedpods of all shapes adorned the trees and the fog almost imperceptibly lifts. Huge trees appeared feathered with fern-like epiphytes. Occasional leaf-lined huts of hunters and fishers appeared as the forest passed by like a movie.

Three days down the river, we camped with the Sangha-Sangha, a group named after the river, and the Baya hunters. They shared their "fish stories" of the animals and the forest. At night we heard the call of the gorillas!

We arrived in Bayanga, a sawmill town out of Joseph Conrad's *Heart of Darkness*. We were received by the village chief and slept in his house by the river. By day we walked with the Pygmies on paths made by forest elephants. In the dense foliage and heavy air, we were able to come quite close to these elegant animals. Forest elephants are generally smaller in body size and have smaller ears than their savanna cousins and have thinner, straighter tusks. We came upon a gorilla nest made simply by bending down the foliage to make a three-meter circular mat on which to sleep.

Getting into the forest by pirogue was much easier than getting a ride out by trucks. After a two-day wait we began bouncing our way back to Bangui. This two-day trip was the last leg of our two-month trek.

In Bangui I sat on the rocky terrace of the fancy Safari hotel on the banks of the Ubangi River, which separates CAR and Zaire. These rocks were a good place for being alone in the midst of the city. Rivers and oceans let the mind flow and grow as big as they are. Water really is the universal solvent as I dissolved my thoughts into the universe.

I watched a lone man paddle swiftly, directly across the top of the rapids loosing nothing to drift. In midstream he intercepted a loose pirogue. Instinctively joining the two boats together, he again paddled the two pirogues upstream in the darkening waters. The *munjus* returned from their picnics in powerboats. In roar and splash they passed. The lone African paddled, gaining on the current and made for the shore where campfire and family waited.

The *munjus* with their mechanized muscle slide across the surface but know not the depth of the African river of life.

I sat in the sunset searching among the whirlpools for a counter current as the sky and water became the same color and drained into gray together. I've loved Africa, the colors, the solid reality of its life as familiar to me now as the trill of a kingfisher and the glow of the fisher's fire.

Duti nzoni. Nzapa bata ala.
Rest well. God guard you all.

2015

Bayanga would become central to my life. I would spend almost ten years in the forest in the southwest tip of CAR jutting between Cameroon and the Congo. I conducted my doctoral work on lowland gorillas, discovering the huge variety of their diets, more than 100 fruits, termites, ants, and the occasional mammal. Lowland gorillas are much more chimp-like than their mountain cousins, and spend much more time in trees and eat way more fruit. As no one had previously worked with gorillas here, we discovered a range extension for this species. I had hoped to habituate the gorillas to my presence so that I could sit with them and have direct observations of their behavior. However, as there was yet no conservation program in this forest, I could not justify habituating the gorillas to people if the next person coming along carried a spear or shotgun. So my work on their feeding ecology was by remote sensing, determining what they ate by what was left behind. I counted and measured lots of stems of wild ginger, the number of termite mounds broken, and collected, dried and sorted through 1,200 fecal samples identifying every fiber and insect part. In number 611, we found rodent hair! I stored these dried fecal samples in newspaper in metal trunks made from old car metal. I shipped these home and got an alarmed call from customs when they read my permit for 1,200 gorillas! The CITES (Convention on the International Trade in Endangered Species) officer in Bangui left off the fecal-sample part.

In fruit eating and arboreal behavior, western lowland gorillas are chimp-like, but very distinctive in termite eating. Whereas chimps delicately fish with stick and blade of grass for termites, gorillas simply rip the mounds off the sides of trees, break them up into fist-size pieces, shake them into their hand, and pop them in to their mouth for a snack!

I put my dissertation on the ten-year plan and set about creating a park and reserve system in this forest in CAR, which would eventually span the entire Congo Basin.

FOURTEEN

African Notes

1978

Reflections . . .just for being

The time for leaving the park (Manovo-Gounda Saint Floris, CAR) had come quite close, and in these last precious days I reflected on what my life has been being here, what I learned, what I saw. Reflections of rainbows and rhinos, elands and elephants ...

-   Of following swiftly and silently the tracks of a rhino, senses alive, eyes and ears awakened, seeking its aura, and there it appears, its majestic muscular mass so firmly planted on the earth, so solid and stoic in its stance ...
-   Of stalking herds of elephants, getting so close I could touch them, channeling my energy into love and not fear, into oneness and not competitiveness ...
-   Of gliding down game trails with my friend and game guard Phillip sweating in the sun, singing African walking chants, being alive ...

- Of walking with my body, becoming personal with the canyons, forests, mountains, and streams; getting there on my own power, feeling my body flow with the land, flying with the feeling of my spirit filling the spaces between the leaves; climbing the highest peaks looking over ancient lava flows, over the continuous river flow, up where the swallows soar and the soul expands to fill the vastness.

Reflections of the sunrise as it rose in stages over the Dongolo Mare, the first glint of light, fading stars, then gray dawn bursting into fuchsia illuminating rippling clouds reflecting on still water. The grunts of hippos as they returned from the nights grazing break the silence and send the pink pelicans circling in the sunrise.

The last few days were spent sitting at familiar salines. Butterflies on the flowers above, warthogs in the mud below, me nestled in a crevice in the solid granite outlook. I was watching one day's life go by in this age-old way of life, the parade of lives, performers passing through this saline stage. I silently watched the butterfly on a flower, the earthbound caterpillar knowing that one day it will fly. A butterfly is but a flying flower, a wind flower (in Sango, *pupulenge*, wind child), spreading the fertility of life from branch to branch. What a connection between butterfly and trees: the larva that feeds on the leaves is the butterfly's bud that blooms to feed the flowers. Butterflies, flowers, rocks, and warthogs, all but different containers of the same light of life, all cells in the universal body, each fulfilling a function; one without the other could not exist. As with us just a brain without a heart will quickly die; a body without the breath of life is an empty shell. Let us unite our brains with our hearts to see and feel the essence of all that exists, let the breath of our bodies and the wind in the trees be one.

Another day and another saline stakeout lying like a lazy lion on a branch of a *Tamarindus* tree entwined by vines, baboons barking below. I was like a bump on a branch, conforming my body to the twist of the tree trunk, transfixed by a twirling leaf until it is plucked by the breeze and floats to the ground. A stream of red army ants advanced determinately along the branch over my shoulder and up the trunk on some mission of their own unknown to me.

The pastel pink of the soil below me was laid bare by hundreds of hooves, the rust-colored laterite (ironstone) boulders balanced precariously, being undermined by elephants digging salt with tusks and trunk. The mud-brown water reflected the blue-gray June sky. A group of hartebeest emerged from the green foliage to drink, emitting throaty mooing sounds. Gray hornbills gave their high-pitched piping calls from the upper branches while below red-cheeked cordon bleus fluttered about the flowering foliage.

It was a still, dreamy day, head on a branch, the sky through the leaves, just being. My camera hung on a branch silent and blind, my binocs loose around my neck. Not a day for mechanized probing and prying, not for thinking and analyzing–just for being.

My time in the parks was coming to an end. We were busy writing reports, getting our last observations in this incredible place that could never be the same. All this ended too quickly, and we were on our way to Bangui. I had an impacted wisdom tooth and was in terrible pain, but I stayed at Koumbala until the last possible moment. Finally, we headed south. I knew that there was an American Baptist Mission in the town of Kaga Bondoro that had a dental clinic. Not only was there a raised ranch compound, there was a full dental clinic, complete with reclining chair, lights, all the tools, and even mood music. The "dentist" wasn't really a dentist, but had read a lot about dentistry and had years of hands-in-mouth experience. He went in, pulled my tooth, with no pain, no fuss, no muss. We were eating chocolate chip cookies, having hot dogs, and watching our language in no time.

We arrived in Bangui, and enjoyed cold beers and hot showers. We were greeted by a response to our "Elephant Research and Protection" proposal we had submitted earlier to funding agencies. The World Wildlife Fund in conjunction with the International Union of the Conservation of Nature (WWF/IUCN) awarded us a grant of $50,000 for this four-year project. This money will be the used for the vehicles for the new team of biologists we trained to continue the elephant work we started. The receipt of this grant gave me a sense of completeness on my part, assuring the continuation of the project. Now I reflect back knowing that I've helped provide for the future of this project and added to the possibility of the survival of elephants and other animals of the park. J. Michael Fay, of *National Geographic* fame, and Richard Ruggerio, of the U.S. Fish and Wildlife Service, got their start in this program.

Now time for our "close of service" (COS) physicals and interviews. My dental COS exam was with Dr. Adio, a very gentle, Iranian Baha'i man, who called me "dear" all the time. This, mind you, was the Carter era and the Iranian hostage situation was in full swing. Dr. Adio examined my wisdom teeth, noticed that one had been removed, and suggested yanking its opposing tooth as it no longer served a function. Sure. It was so easy in Kaga Bondoro. I don't think that Carter or the hostage scene had anything to do with it, but he grabbed on to the tooth with pliers, seemed to put his foot wedged against my chest, and yanked, turned, twisted, and pulled, until a bloody fragment of a tooth emerged. He said he went back in to check for remaining bits and broken bones, was satisfied, and stitched me up.

The pain. More codeine! Can't work, can't concentrate. Went back to Dr. Adio, he said, "Dear, dear everything is fine." I flew to Paris on the codeine express and went to the first dentist I could find. He looked in, and plucked the half-inch fragments of jawbone that had been scissoring up through my gums for two weeks!

Going to Paris was not our first choice for leaving Bangui with style. We first wanted to leave from the park's northern border with Sudan and go through Juba and up the Nile. The border with Sudan was closed, as tough times were beginning in that part of the world.

Our next choice was the river boat from Bangui, down the Ubangi and Congo Rivers to the coast. Another good neighbor, Zaire had closed its borders with CAR–can't get there from here.

Reflections of well-being in Bangui as I was with my heart friend Clements. The sun through the white overcast rainy season sky reflected on the smooth, deep, rich darkness of her skin. The pulse of life beats close to the surface of her veins and courses through Africa, not yet completely covered by the curtain of civilization.

This beat has been transfused into my being, and even as I boarded the plane for Paris I know it will carry me on through the dance of my life.

So, after a flight to Paris and a good dentist, Bruce and I were off to the top of Europe, the Tour du Mount Blanc.

2015

I returned to Manovo-Gounda Saint Floris National Park in 1984 with Tom McShane from WWF-U.S. and his wife, Erica. I was starting the Dzanga-Sangha Project and doing concurrent PhD studies on gorilla feeding ecology with my friend J. Michael Fay. My work as project director for Dzanga-Sangha was funded by WWF, and as the WWF-funded work in Manovo-Gounda Saint Floris National park was drawing to a close, we transferred the old Toyota Land Cruiser from MGSF to Dzanga-Sangha.

Mike and I met Erica and Tom at the airport. The next day, we left for a trip to Bayanga. We made it as far as Yaloké, and the old truck broke down. Mike hitched a ride back to Bangui to buy parts to repair the truck, and I treated Tom and Erica to tea and bread in the Yaloké market. Erica broke a baguette, was about to dunk it in her tea, and then noticed dark pellets in the bread–goat droppings. She held it up in disgust, and I said, "What's wrong, that's just Central African raisin bread!"

We made our visit to Bayanga, then my wife, (now ex) Rita, our two year old daughter, Deva, and I, with Tom and Erica, started the cross-country voyage from the far southern tip of CAR to the northern extremes, staying in missions along the way. Tom was on a project with UNESCO to evaluate MGSF as a potential World Heritage Site. Finally we got to MGSF, but we saw few animals. I said, "Just wait until we get to the Gounda Valley. It will be teaming with wildlife."

As we exited the *Terminalia*-wooded savanna and arrived on the Gounda plains, the first animals we saw were 20 camels mounted by Sudanese with heavy automatic weapons and bullet belts strapped across their chests. They had just about terminated the elephants and rhinos in northern CAR and were now killing anything that moved for meat to load on their camels to haul back home. We drove on most of the day and reached the Gounda camp and told the French man running the park about what we witnessed. The next day a French military plane arrived and dispatched soldiers to deal with the poachers.

In the meantime, I took Tom et al. around the Gounda region, up to Mare Gata and saw the vast potential that this region held. At one point, I had Tom drive while I sat on the roof holding Deva tightly in my arms as we drove slowly on the road along the floodplains. We stopped to see a sleepy pride of lions along the road. As we pulled up, the right wheel of the truck slipped off the axel, the truck listed to a sudden stop, and Deva and I slid directly in front of the lions. I felt like I was offering my firstborn to them! Their reaction: they woke up and looked annoyed that we had disturbed their sleep. I put Deva in the truck, and Tom and I rethreaded the stripped wheel bearing enough to hold, looking over our shoulders at the lions while we worked, and we managed to limp the truck back to camp.

Tom, Erica, Rita, and Deva flew back to Bangui with the French military plane, and I waited for my friend Nassif, a Lebanese mechanic in Bangui, to drive up with parts and tools to fix the truck. When Tom got back to Washington, he sent me funds for a new vehicle.

Elephants in the north of CAR have been reduced by about 90 percent. The western black rhino is now extinct. Everything that moves is potential bush meat. As you fly over a forest, the vast expanse of green is inspiring, but underneath, the forest may be empty of its wildlife. Wise use of wildlife could mean food security for Central Africans, as well as cultural security for people like the BaAka, whose lives depend on an intact forest. As I said earlier, the bush meat crisis in now the leading cause of biodiversity loss in Africa. The bush meat trade amounts to over a million tons per year, the equivalent of a billion hamburgers per year. Before we leave Africa in this volume, I'll leave you with some facts and figures on this wildlife trade.

The Bush Meat Crisis in the Congo Basin

- The Bush meat crisis in the Congo Basin is a human health and food security issue, an economic and political issue as well as an urgent ecological issue. The bush meat trade is the leading cause of biodiversity loss in the Congo Basin and is motored by an accelerating logging industry and growing human population.

- Approximately 20 million people depend on the resources of the forest for food, materials, and shelter. Consumption of bush meat is estimated to be about a million metric tons per year, and as human populations are expected to double in the next 25 years, if no alternatives are found, it will spell extinction of most wildlife species and result in a food crisis and ecological crisis of massive proportions.

- The bush meat problem covers both subsistence hunting and commercial hunting. Commercial hunting supplies urban markets in the African countries themselves, and even serves consumption needs abroad where there are large expatriate populations of Africans.

- If the demand for bush meat continues to grow as expected, and consumers do not switch to the meat of domestic animals, we can expect that apes and most large-bodied forest mammals will be eradicated from the forest, throughout much of the region.

- Projections of future logging trends suggest that an estimated 7o percent of the region's forests could be lost by 2040 unless large-scale changes aimed at conserving the forest and the livelihoods of its native people are taken now. Logging operations open up the forest, creating paths and access that are then used by hunters and trappers. The animals killed are often then transported to the urban centers on vehicles belonging to the logging company.

- The chimpanzee and other primates have been suggested as potential vectors for the emerging diseases related to HIV/AIDs and the recent outbreaks of Ebola have been linked to the handling and eating of wildlife.

- For forest people like the BaAka Pygmies, whose cultural, physical, and spiritual life depends on an intact forest, forest and wildlife depletion means cultural extinction as well.

- At the local level, bush meat is a survival issue. Simple subsistence is no longer possible. All communities and all families are part of the cash economy, however modestly. Families must pay school fees, buy medicines, and purchase salt, sugar, soap, and kerosene.

- Civil conflict both stems from and creates resource degradation. Increasingly, military weapons are used by commercial poachers, especially for large animals such as elephants. Most illegal shooting of bush meat still takes place with shotguns using shells manufactured in Congo or Nigeria. Pressure should be brought to close these factories and limit the availability of hunting apparatus such as steel cables used for snares.

- Logging companies are showing an increasing willingness to collaborate, especially on reduction of bush meat hunting on their concessions. Examples are the work of Wildlife Conservation Society in Congo and of WWF with a Malaysian company near the Minkebe Reserve in Gabon. These methods hold promise for replication throughout the priority regions.

- WWF is working with governments and private railway companies in Cameroon and Gabon to reduce transport of bush meat.

- In terms of GDP, all sub-Saharan countries allocate a larger percentage of their budgets to national protected area systems than do either the United States or Canada.

- The Yaoundé Heads of State Summit and Declaration have raised the political commitment to conservation in the Congo Basin by a quantum leap and has presented a unique opportunity to establish a coherent conservation plan for the Congo Basin. This plan calls for a regional network of trans-border and other protected areas, a halt to uncontrolled and illegal logging and hunting, and a greater integration of local populations and the private sector in forest management.

FIFTEEN

World Wanderings–Alpine Adventures

1978

After Africa, a week of Paris's monuments and metros moved me to move myself out to the mountains. Bruce and I hopped the train heading southeast. Our destination: Gland, Switzerland, for a visit with the folks of the World Wildlife Fund/International Union for the Conservation of Nature (WWF/IUCN) to discuss the details of our African elephant research project funded by them. Then we were off on a two-week walk in the Alps, the Tour du Mont Blanc.

In the French countryside, wheat fields and vineyards replaced African manioc and millet, white Charlet cattle replaced the long-horned zebu of the Fulani nomads and the manicured, fenced-off landscape replaced the wild expanses of the African savanna. The pines and poplars, maples and willows, birch and elderberries brought me one step closer to home. Red tiled-roofed, whitewashed chalets surrounded by chestnut trees, the occasional old stone church with spires and statues, brought the past to the present and the rhythm of the rails rocked me into dreamland.

We spent the night in the youth hostel in Geneva, then took the train the next day around Lac Léman to Gland, Switzerland, to visit the WWF/

IUCN headquarters. With our African affairs finished, we headed for the Alps.

The trains got smaller as the mountains got taller. Three short rides through farmland nestled between the hills brought us to the Swiss Alpine village of La Roche. During the ride from La Roche to Saint-Gervais we had a *casse-croûte* snack of bread and cheese. Purple joe-pye weed and white Queen Anne's' lace brightened the fallow fields along the track side.

The train climbed slower and slower around the bends up the mountains, and suddenly the snowcapped splendor of Mont Blanc appeared against the blue Alpine sky. The train let us off at Les Houches with a panorama of peaks patched with snow and laced with clouds. The dark pines gave way to gray rock ridges with a backdrop of clear skies.

We walked through the village and began the Tour du Mont Blanc. The afternoon's walk took us through woods of birch and maples, cow pasture clearings with the peaks of Mont Lachat, Aiguille (Needle) du Goûter, the Dôme du Goûter, Mont Maudit, and Mont Blanc Peak, at 15,623 feet, the highest point in Europe, towering above. Below the village of Les Houches lay nestled in the valley along the Arregron River. We set up camp at 4,800 feet in a cow pasture filled with pink fireweed, yarrow, wild geranium, red clover, and buttercups.

The brilliance of the setting sun advanced up the slopes until only the snowcapped summits remained aglow in golden light for a few magnificent minutes, then dusk settled into the Alps. The cowbell wind chimes reminded me of African xylophones–from the Alps to African, *pas loin*, not all that far away.

We finished our morning packing as the sun peeked over the peaks, and the rays extended down through the misty valley and brightened the rocky ridges all around.

A long steep climb through the pines put us in an Alpine meadow full of flowers, the ring of cowbells riding the wind. The cows nuzzled up to us, licking us with raspy tongues, the crisp clear air filled with the sweetness of their odor.

As we climbed higher, more and more peaks appeared behind the others. Marbled glaciers and scoured rock extended down into the higher valleys. The steep, steady climbs in the light Alpine air were difficult for us since we had adapted to the hot African savanna.

I was greeted at the Col du Tricot at 7,000 feet by the tinkling bells of sheep grazing in the mountain meadows around the ruins of an old chalet. These dry stone walls once housed shepherds as well as French refugees in their resistance in the Second World War. The long continuous climb ended abruptly here with the far side descending sharply. We descended the

Tour du Mount Blanc.

2,000 feet into the valley of the Miage at the foot of the Dômes de Miage. Water pouring out of the glaciers 1,000 feet up formed falls and torrents tumbling through the valley. We washed quickly in the icy water just as the sun set behind Mont Truc. Again the air was filled with the charm of cowbells from the grassy slopes.

In the little village, the shale that makes the mountains makes the houses, too. The red flag cross of the Haute-Savoie district waved over the slate-roofed chalet that housed a small restaurant and refuge for hikers and skiers. This trail, with its challenging climbs and spectacular scenery, is served by rustic refuges similar to the Appalachian Mt. Trail Club huts in the White Mountains of New Hampshire. It also passed through small Alpine villages where you can buy homemade bread and cheese from farming families. If you prefer to carry money instead of heavy gear, you can eat

From Africa to the Alps.

and sleep in the refuges and lighten the load. We, with little money, carried everything we needed for Alpine camping, the weight of which made the long climbs longer.

Never have I camped in more magnificent surrounding, but I've said that before, and I'll surely say it again. Wherever I am is the most beautiful place on earth and the only place on the earth to be at that moment.

The next morning's meander brought us down another 1,500 feet into the valley of Contamines-Montjoie. It happened to be the day of the Fête de L'Étape, an Alpine celebration. Traditional music from the Haute-Savoie, dancers in original costumes frolicked in the cool sunshine. Mandolin, fiddle, and accordion music echoed among the surrounding peaks.

From the valley we climbed a continuous 5,000 feet to the Col de Bonhomme, crossing patches of snow, skirting glaciers, and drinking from their flowing substance. At 8,000 feet, peaks towered another 6,000 feet above us. The high-pitched whistle of a marmot pierced.

Tiny forget-me-nots snuggled amongst the rocks, buttercups and blue-bells–the Alps in bloom. I sat on the windward side of the cairn on the Col de Croix de la Bonhomme. Below the massive stone refuge stood perched on a cliff. In one direction the jagged cliffs formed a sharp outline against the sky, in the other they blended into the misty clouds.

It's so life-giving to be atop a mountain where the solid meets the air, where the breath of the breeze forms all, where the breath of life fills all. It is a place where the physical meets the ethereal; where the spirit reaches from its earthly trappings and soars the silver sky.

From my repos at the cairn we climbed another 1,000 feet across snow and loose shale. I was a bit bewildered for a moment as to where the trail went next. To the right and left were sheer cliffs, in front a steep slope covered with snow. Boot tracks in the slushy snow gave it away–straight down.

The 6,000 feet we gained through the day's climb, we had to descend again this afternoon. So down, skiing on boots through snow and soggy loose shale, knee knocking, thigh thumping 3,300 feet to the valley and the Ville des Glaciers (Glacier City). The Ville des Glaciers is a tiny mountain village of a dozen stone buildings and four long stone barracks that once served as a military training site before being destroyed in the Second World War. Most of the buildings shelter cows, only a few house humans. Three barns served as refuges for hikers, and a family ran a small restaurant selling home-cooked soups, omelets, bread, cheese, and wine. We partook of a *petit repast* for the flavor of the food and the flavor of the country folk.

The following day's long, cold climb in the clouds brought me to the Col de Seine and the French and Italian border. At the top the clouds cleared, and jagged peaks and pinnacles appeared all around. The clouds rolled back, and a little collection of people huddled around the leeward side of the cairn. French, Italians, Germans, Swiss, and Americans shivered and shared experiences, bread and cheese.

We left the trail in the Italian valley of Courmayeur to head to the Italian National Park of the Gran Paradiso in hopes of photographing chamois and ibex, two Alpine goat-like critters. The bus ride took us through a valley of terraced hillsides, and each town was dominated by an old stone castle perched on a hill-top.

In Aosta we had a three-hour lay-over between buses, giving us time to explore the 2,000-year-old Roman ruins. We saw huge old Roman stone arches built without mortar, the ruins of a Roman theater, and every step in time from 100 BC to the present represented in the architecture. The next bus took us up and up a winding, incredibly narrow road along the sheer side of a mountain dropping down 2,000 feet into a rushing white glacial river, traversed by an ancient Roman bridge. Ribbon-like cascades crashed down 3,000 feet from the towering ridge. We arrived in Cogne after sunset and inconspicuously hiked across a cow field under cover of darkness to camp next to the river. In spite of the chill of the evening air and the iciness of the glacial river, I plunged and splashed for a long 20 second bath.

It came to my attention how much I'm attracted to roofs while traveling, noticing materials used and the methods of application, from grass to corrugated metal of Central Africa to slate and tile of France and Italy. Some of the roofs of the old houses in the Alpine villages were huge slate slabs with boulders on top to hold it in place. One I saw was of planks made from splitting a hollow tree. These curved planks were imbricated and held in place by logs and boulders. After many months of fiddling around on roofs applying shingles and doing repairs in college and after, I appreciate creative roofing.

When we arrived at the Gran Paradiso National Park, we looked to see where the tourist trails took off and went in the opposite direction hoping to find a secluded spot and the shy chamois. We climbed a steep streambed up 2,000 feet to a grassy ridge with larch trees and the source of the stream forming a canyon with jagged cliffs. Grass, water, and rock: a perfect chamois sanctuary. We scanned the cliffs with our binocs, and there in a patch of green was a group of chamois.

A pair of young golden eagles were trying out their wings supervised by an adult, their shrill cry filling the space. A red-shouldered kestrel did some aerobatics around the walls, and a tiny merlin streaked through on pointed wings.

We spent the next day perched in the pines watching the chamois feed and frolic on the cliffs. Higher up came the rumble of rocks falling caused by two chamois chasing each other, making daring leaps on little ledges until they found themselves stranded, afraid to go up or down. Here they spent the day until they found the nerve to make the ten-meter jump to flatter ground.

Another day was passed clinging to a crevasse on the shady side of the cliff behind a stunted larch tree, shivering in the icy wind waiting for a chamois to saunter by. Their presence was usually made known by the sound of sliding shale in their path. First one, then three more of the masked little elf-like antelopes bounced by grazing and hopping from rock to rock. The family of golden eagles rode the wind around the canyon and over the cliffs.

We left the Gran Paradiso National Park and bussed back to the Mont Blanc trail at Arnuva, Italy. I bought a loaf of bread as large as a football, found a boulder to block the wind, and snacked on stale bread and apple juice, seeking the warmth of the last rays of sun.

From the icy Arnuva valley we climbed toward the sun, up near the glaciers where the sheep bells rang in the Swiss-Italian wind. At the Col Ferret we re-entered Switzerland. Just over the border, high in the mountains, two custom agents asked to see our passports. From there it was down again to the Swiss valley of Ferret where the Alpine farm folks were raking up their hay with oversized wooden rakes and stuffing it into lofts for winter insulation and livestock feed.

The view from the valley of the ragged, rocky ridges and their pointed peaks and pinnacles reminded me of the old-time cathedrals we visited in France. Notre Dame, Chartres, and others, with their steeples and spires, seem to be inspired by these mountains. It seems that people in their lofty aspirations seek to imitate the majesty of the mountains as the dwelling place of the gods.

It seems to me more valid to take oneself to the mountaintops, to stand exposed to the wind, the sun, exposed to oneself, naked to the earth and the sky, to creation, than to carve up the mountains for marble to try to re-create these true cathedrals already in place through the millennia for the minds and spirits of people.

We rambled along a jeep path leading through mountain cattle mead-ows out of the valley of Poya. We set our packs down and grazed on the roadside raspberries, blueberries, and strawberries. The woods along this stretch were so much like the pinewoods back home, with moist mosses and the damp rich odor. We sat using our packs for pillows, eating berries while the shadows rose up the opposite mountains. Like two hobos we sat there, so comfortable in our mountain paradise. Wherever we set our packs down became our home. All we needed was on our back. When it got cold we could pull out an extra shirt. When we were hungry there were berries

Cowbells in the Alps.

on the path and rice in the pack. For those moments we were free to wander, to roam with packs, boots, and tent, the world our home.

Our last day was one of cowbells in the clouds and then back into France. We ended our Tour du Mont Blanc in the town of Chamonix. Here Bruce and I parted–him off to visit friends in Germany and Norway, me back to Paris to await my sister Lynn for our trip to East Africa, India, and all in between.

2015

I was to return to Switzerland, France, and Italy many times over the years with WWF. The WWF Secretariat, WWF-International, is based in Gland, Switzerland, as is the International Union for the Conservation of Nature (IUCN). WWF is a bit like a federation, with independent national organizations in 26 countries, such as WWF-U.S., WWF France, etc., including Brazil and Indonesia. The CEOs of the National Organizations make up the International Board, and, they, along with Country Representatives from the 55 Program Offices, scattered across the globe, establish the global framework program, which all support financially and technically. It is a complicated model, but the only truly international conservation organization working worldwide for the conservation of nature. This model allows WWF to fundraise globally, and it has a membership base of over five million members. WWF-U.S., the largest National Organization, has 1.2 million members, who all support the program and who all vote. However, even with this broad U.S. support for international wildlife conservation, our track record in the U.S. seems to be lagging behind in terms of addressing global issues such as climate change. Our European colleagues are far ahead of us, and WWF-U.S. and other groups have their work cut out for them on these issues to bring the U.S. along, vying with China for the status of largest polluter.

SIXTEEN

World Wanderings–Greece

1978

On the road again after too long a stay in Paris, now with my new traveling partner, my sweet sister Lynn. We caught the Magic Bus, paying $54 each for the two-and-a half day ride east to Athens. As we crossed the now familiar French landscape, our burly bus driver sang Greek love songs. Back we went, now by bus into the Alps that I so recently visited by boot and backpack.

After a wakeful night we awoke in Italy, then shortly we passed into Yugoslavia. We changed our Italian lira into Yugoslavian dinar at the border. We rolled on past scrubby dark pines, locust, and birch, which bespoke poor soil. The terraced hillsides were planted in corn, grapes, mustard, and vegetable patches. Occasionally, buckwheat was planted to enrich the plots. The mustard is picked and hung upside down on thatched-roofed drying racks. On we went through Yugoslavian farms and towns, through the mounting hills and winding country roads. In the light, dreary drizzle the greens faded into grays and I faded off into dreams.

On the wet windy roads, the going was slow, the air filled with blaring Greek music and cigarette smoke from our Greek hosts. The noise, smoke and perpetual motion of the bus was a bit unpleasant, but I had a pleasant person, Lynn, to share it with.

The bus drove on past fields of sunflowers bowing their heads like so many Buddhist monks to the sun. Roadside watermelon wagons were tended by women wearing babushkas, long skirts, and sweaters or men in mackinaws leaning against a tractor or wagon waiting for customers.

We drove to Belgrade in the drizzling dusk after a day through the flat cornfields of Yugoslavia, leaving the impression of dreariness, desolation, and oppression.

We woke up in Greece with the morning sun over the Aegean Sea to the east and mountains to the west. A huge old stone castle perched on a hill guarded the mountain pass, as country folk rode donkeys down the road. Tiny roadside shrines protected the traveler, and the gloom of Yugoslavia was behind us.

The bus wound up through the rocky hills past the Spring of Venus and Mt. Olympus. Men herded small flocks of sheep into the hills from grass-roofed, stone and log barns. Cotton fields and olive and almond orchards enriched this Arizona-like landscape.

As we moved south, the terrain became more semi desert, with hills of blue-gray rock patched with dark green scrub and a red tinge throughout. These somber hills contrasted with the bright straw-colored wheat fields below.

We finally arrived in Athens and checked into the crowded noisy youth hostel. From within, Athens was another huge overcrowded busy modern city. From above at the ancient ruins of the Acropolis, where the winds whistle through the age-old pillars, one could almost feel the presence of the gods and goddesses to which the temples were dedicate. Below the Acropolis was the ancient agora village and temple and the old town of

Plaka. Plaka, with its rooftop gardens and narrow stone alleys, was alive with bouzouki music and dancing by night. By day hawkers sold their wares. Old women, usually widows dressed in black, wove sweaters and shawls from hand-spun wool. The flea market stretched on through cobbled streets, selling everything from army surplus to ancient artifacts, replicas of vases and remnants and relics from bygone days. And everywhere there was the music and bickering of the Greeks, who seem to be carrying on a constant argument, yelling at each other from shop to shop.

At night we watched traditional dances at the Dora Santory Theater at the base of the Acropolis. The music, shouts, and stomps echoed through the hills. After the dances we climbed a hill and looked across to the changing light show on the Acropolis, bathed in the natural light of the full moon.

On Nikis Street we booked cheap passage to the islands and bought black market student cards for reduced rates on future voyages. We boarded bus, metro, and finally boat to take us to the islands. At 11:30 P.M. we cast off under full moon toward Naxos, spreading our sleeping bags on the upper deck in the fresh night sea breeze. At 5:30 A.M. we docked and thinking we'd arrived at our destination we disembarked half asleep. As the gangplank closed we awoke to the fact that this island was Paros not Naxos so we unrolled our mats on the beach and watched the harbor come to life.

As the sun appeared over the dry terraced hills, the moon sank into the sea, and rocky cliffs and islands rose out of the dark blue water. The tangerine sky was etched by windmill and boat masts and reflected on the rippling waters of the harbor. Gradually, the other beach squatters awoke to the island day.

Blue Byzantine domes capped whitewashed temples overlooking the sea. The square Arab-style buildings were also bathed in sunrise orange, the round arched verandas bringing grace to the angular.

We caught the noon boat out of Paros. The big motor churned the marble Mediterranean waters. The brown hills of Naxos appeared out of the blue, and the whitewashed town stood like a beacon on the hill over the harbor. We wandered up through the alleys and arches, the white walls hung with purple morning glories, orange cats basking in the shade. Old women wrapped in black knitted with gnarled hands in the tiny, neat houses. The crosses of the many churches stood against the blue sky. Religious symbols adorned every arch and doorway.

We took the bus to the Agia Anna beach. While the driver and Greek passengers were in a heated discussion, we rounded arid hills spiked with yucca and cactus. Stone walls crisscrossed the landscape, holding in the few goats, cows, and mules the sparse vegetation would support. An occasional old-timer would pass riding sidesaddle on mule, the wooden saddle strung with baskets and sacks. The small, square, flat-roofed stone houses amongst the dry terrain looked Mexican. The narrow strip of pavement ended and we continued down a dirt track with 15-foot-tall cane grass on each side until we emerged on the sea. Stacks of potatoes waited on docks to be transported by boat to the mainland.

We walked along the shore barefoot with our backpacks. The two-tone aquamarine and indigo Mediterranean lapped at our feet. We passed a hilltop church and set up camp two kilometers down the beach. I felt weightless in the salty sea and meditated at the water's edge as the sun lowered toward the hills across the way. The fine, faint silhouette of the distant mountains and the sharp circle of molten colors of the sun was like an Oriental design.

I lay naked in the sand by the crystal sea. A man with a cactus face and desert skin brought us prickly pear cactus fruits, which he skillfully peeled avoiding the spines. His loose faded blue denim bloomers billowed in the breeze as he led his donkey away amongst the nude sunbathers. A few short years brought these people from potato planters to tourist traders. As the old generation dies, where is the place for the new?

We made our way back to Naxos and Pireas under a waning moon. As I looked up I saw the outline of the fullness behind the shadows and knew that even in these times of changes, wholeness will emerge once again.

Now we wait in the Athens airport for our flight to Cairo for our Nile adventures.

2015

Having a passion for mountains and oceans, I got a long needed dose of each in these two legs of my post-Peace Corps CAR travels. After majoring in marine biology and hiking the Appalachian Trail, I ended up in CAR, as far from the mountains or the ocean that one can get on earth! It was nice to be back.

In recent years, Greece, now a European Union member, has gone through economic hardships. During our visit, we were still living out of backpacks, and we wouldn't have noticed!

SEVENTEEN

World Wanderings–Egypt

After Athens, we cruised into Cairo, Air Egypt, and touched down with a loud thud on Egyptian terrain. The heaviness of our landing hung with us for most of our 12-day stay in Egypt. We collected our backpacks and made our way through the robed, turbaned squatters on the sidewalks, always on guard for quick hands at the backs of our packs. After asking several police, we found the right bus to take us to town. Fortunately at this late-night hour it wasn't the crowded fiasco we'd heard of. We got seated, and since all the passengers were staring at us anyway, we got them involved in finding our direction, reading the Cairo map, and got some broken-English tourist guides as we forged through the crowded streets. We changed buses at Tahrir Square and finally arrived at the Al Gaman Bridge and the Cairo youth hostel.

Now I've slept in some funky places in my time, but the Cairo youth hostel was a dirty dump that was somehow undeservedly spared the demolition team's doom. From the greasy window of the room I shared with eight cigarette-smoking, radio-playing Egyptian students, I got my first view of the Nile River, through the torrent of traffic, the blare of a kung fu movie, and the unsettled silt of desert dust.

We stayed but one-bedbug-bite scratching night at the hostel and then moved to an Italian-run pensione. We paid a higher price for cleanliness, calmness, breakfast, and one other home-cooked meal per day. The only complaint was that the home-cooked carrot and potato meal was the same each day.

By day we walked through the dirt and crowds of crumbling Cairo with the continuous chorus of car horns and police whistles, exhaust, dust, and insults constantly spew in our faces. Cairo felt like a depressing, dying city, collapsing into the desert dust. In every alley, beneath bridges and walkways the smells of urine and excrement foul the filthy air.

At the old Arab bazaar of Khan el-Khalili, hawkers and hashish dealers vied for our attention. "Come into my shop, smell my perfumes, no charge for looking–change your money? Good rate today-want hashish, good stuff, etc., etc." Sacks of exotic spices and herbs, jars of pure Egyptian perfumes, and handmade metalwork as well as the ever-present array of plastic shoes and Western clothes filled the shops. In the back alleys of the bazaar away from the teaming crowds, the sunlight through the burlap roof filtered the dusty darkened air. Here the spices were ground, and oils blended into age-old scents. Women in mourning dressed in black sold dates and guavas in the street, tiny donkeys and Arabian ponies pulled huge wooden-wheeled wagons.

The Egyptian Museum in Cairo was crammed full of fantastic artifacts of ancient Egypt. The King Tut exhibit was exposed in all its splendor, and thousands of signs and symbols of these ancient sun worshippers were seen.

We went out of Cairo and as abruptly as the wooded Nile valley became desert, a new, old Egypt emerged. The three tall pyramids appeared above the sands, and I felt the deep solemnness of the place in spite of the crude camel drivers wanting me to ride their camel or horse; or spend five minutes in the dunes with them; or the smooth sultan upon his steed saying "Take a picture of Moses by the pyramid only 2 LE"; the mystic vibrations were felt in spite of the tourists' graffiti inside and out and their shouts within the sacred halls and burial chambers. Lynn and I managed to find ourselves alone in the heart of the Pyramid of Cheops in the empty vault. We meditated here in the middle of this place of pyramid power and could feel ourselves rising toward the center, drawn to the point of the pyramid where the mystical eye of ancient Egyptians gazed into eternity.

The sun set behind the Sphinx and the surrounding sands turned golden as gorgeous Arabian horses galloped across the desert dunes. Camels did their soft shoe back to the stables, and peace settled into the pyramids. We wandered around the town, Giza, at dusk. We stopped to admire an Arabian stallion, and Lynn was invited for a ride on this majestic horse. As she pranced around on this magnificent animal I sat with a group of men, the aristocratic owner of the horse, and drank tea. They all smoked tobacco through a huge hookah pipe, and we ate five-cent falafels sitting on soda cases on the sidewalk and talked with many more sincerely friendly folks here a bit away from the tourist haunts.

We boarded the luxurious first-class train to Luxor–at half-price student fares–and passed out of Cairo through groves of date palms and lush fields of veggies, miles of millet, corn, rice, cotton, and sugarcane. All methods from hoe to oxen to tractor were used to plow, and water flows through irrigation ditches with pumps powered by oxen. Camels and mules were beasts of burden and are often seen buried beneath mounds of millet stalks.

Hanging in the haze at the edge of the green Nile Valley looms the Sahara. We passed through towns of mud brick, baked brick, and cement houses. Some roofless houses were shaded by millet stalks, which also provide ready fuel. Kilns in the fields baked bricks, the fires fueled by millions of millet stalks. The spires of Moslem mosques and domes and crosses of Coptic Christian churches dominated the towns.

The next morning we managed to find a mellow man among the multitude of donkey dealers to guide us on a daylong donkey ride through the desert to the Valley of the Queens, Valley of the Kings, the Tombs of the Nobles, Ramses Temple, etc. We crossed the Nile by ferry, where the ticket taker tried to take us for twice the price, mounted our tiny donkeys on packsaddles padded with rags, and were off. From the river we passed through fields of sugarcane and millet to the ornately carved Colossi of Ramses decorated with designs of divinities and hieroglyphics. Abruptly, the greenery ended, and we entered the bone-dry rocky rubble of the desert. Up the sunbaked shale, we entered into the holy hills housing the tombs of the ancient queens and kings. In these hallowed hills, great halls were carved and inscribed with divine directions to the deceased to enter the afterlife, to guide them to the gods. The inhabitant's history was written in the walls in hieroglyphics. The treasures of the tombs have been pilfered or put into museums along with the mummies that inhabited them. Only in Tut's tomb did the golden inner casket remain. Another kind of grave robber remained greedily awaiting at each tomb to guide tourists, read the writing on the walls, and sell fake artifacts all for a little baksheesh.

In the heat of the desert day we climbed out of the Kings' valley to our donkeys, circled the crumbling cliffs of the valley rim, and descended powdery paths to visit the nobles' tombs and Rameses' Temple. Not one inch of the great rock walls of Rameses' Temple remained uncarved, depicting the life history of this ruler.

After Ramses' Temple we trotted back to the Nile, drank tea with our guide, ferried back to Luxor, and the next day made the long train ride back to Cairo.

Egypt–a land of many lessons for us. A land once flourishing but perhaps stifled by the rigidity of Islam and conflicts between religious groups. It seemed that as the resistance to change causes the crumbling, the desire for change causes the crowding in the capital city of Cairo. It's with these contrasts, as sharp as the river in the desert, that the courageous, powerful and popular President Sadat must lead the country.

The trials of Egypt also served to test our traveling techniques, to see what we can live with and live without, to move us closer together as we move on.

Tonight we fly to Nairobi, Kenya, to experience another aspect of Africa.

2015

This was written one week before the assassination of Sadat. My later trips to Egypt were quite different. After the shooting of tourists, security at the sites became extremely tight. No more donkey rides through the desert. Now your bus takes you to the paved parking lots at the Valley of the Kings, and you are ushered by heavily armed military. No more men with mirrors lighting the tunnels for baksheesh! The Arab Spring brought a new image of Tahrir Square, and hoped for a new image for the country.

EIGHTEEN

World Wanderings–Kenya

1978

The moon was in its first quarter and Venus shone in the blue-black sky and the cool clean air of East Africa. Nairobi, a city of flowering trees, singing birds, clean and light was a welcome contrast to Cairo. Cheerful helpful people reflected the clear temperate feeling of this tropical paradise.

We took a bus from the airport to the Nairobi youth hostel and met David, the Kenyan hostel warden. David took a great deal of personal responsibility to make the Nairobi youth hostel the best I've seen. Chores were done on a communal basis, keeping the place in order and giving guests some direct personal involvement in the hostel. I was struck by the contrast of David's dedication compared to the corruption and entrenched irresponsibility of many Central African officials.

We spent a few days around town eating curries at the many Indian restaurants. East Indians formed a commercial class in East African much like the Hausa and Lebanese merchants in West Africa.

I visited the Nairobi headquarters of the African Wildlife Leadership Foundation and talked elephants with fellow researchers from Kenya and

Tanzania. I called a correspondent of mine during the last year in our Central African elephant project planning, Dr. Iain Douglas-Hamilton, and we had lunch with him and his wife Oria. They are the authors of *Among the Elephants* and the chief champions of elephant protection in Africa. Sitting in their sunny garden, we discussed the African-wide elephant situation, especially the Central African scene.

After these few eventful days in Nairobi, we rented a Suzuki 4x4 truck and headed toward Maasai Mara National Reserve. Not far from Nairobi we rounded the escarpment and descended into the Rift Valley. In this broad basin we began seeing giraffes, Thompson's and Grant's gazelles, and Cooke's hartebeest all along the roadside. This co-existence of wildlife and human activity was the first I've seen outside a park in Africa or the world. The pavement ended and the road turned dusty. We bounced along through the semi desert acacia scrub country past bead-and-blanket-clad Maasai tending their cattle carrying their long spears, clubs, and bows. A sign of Maasai beauty seems to be elongated earlobes stretched by huge silver earrings. Sometimes their earlobes are looped over the top of their ears.

The marvelous Maasai Mara Reserve–the rolling hills were teaming with tens of thousands of wildebeest, moving steadily south, with hundreds of zebra, gazelle, hartebeest, topi, occasional elephants and elusive cheetahs.

From Maasai Mara we moved north to Lake Naivasha and the flamingo-filled Lake Nakuru. Both are birdwatcher's paradise, and Naivasha hosts a pair of lammergeyer (bearded vultures).

We drove the dirt roads across rolling plains past grazing gazelle into the far west town of Maru Moro. To the west were the hills of Aberdare National Park, home of the famous Tree House Hotel; to the east the ridge of Mt. Kenya was indistinguishable from the clouds. We left the plains and climbed to the gate of Mt. Kenya National Park. Up and up we drove our suffering Suzuki on the winding roads to the meteorological station at 10,000 feet. We booked a cabin and slowly got acclimated to the altitude while watching the birds and fantastic montane forest vegetation. At dusk below our cabin a pair of sitatunga, a swamp-loving antelope, came grazing in the meadow. The next morning we slopped our way up to 13,000 feet through what's called the "vertical bog," a steep muddy bog in the montane forest up to tree line and out first view of the snow-studded peaks.

We reached the ridge at 14,000 feet, going from savanna to snow line. Here we had lunch as the clouds obscured the 17,000-foot peaks. The savanna full of farms, fields and wildlife unfolded below. I am fortunate to have seen the flow of Africa–from the interior forests to the coral coast, from the desert sands to the snowy heights.

We climbed back down through the buffalo bogs, the eucalyptus, and pine forest to the flowering euphorbia, cactus, and flat-topped thorn bushes of the savanna. The snowy peaks of Mt. Kenya glowed in the morning sun. Grassy hills were dotted with sheep, broad valleys and terraced hills plowed by tractor or oxen. Unlike Central Africa, with her small villages and towns surrounded by vast bush, much of Kenya's population is distributed on large farms, former British holdings subdivided by the Africans after independence. People wait with milk cans, others with sacks of potatoes at the roadside to sell to the agricultural cooperative.

We entered the thickly forested country of the Meru district and headed east on the newly repaired road to the Meru National Park. At the Meru lodge, we had a cold Tusker beer on the cool veranda overlooking a waterhole and a spectacle of 70 elephants, as well as zebra, oryx, waterbuck, gazelle, baboons, and a barrage of birds.

We moved on in the heat of the day. Ostrich trotted down the dusty track ahead of us. We booked a $2-per-night *banda* (cabin) on a little stream and watched the birds from our shady front porch.

Meru hosted Kenya's only white or square-lipped rhinos, six in all, under constant guard. Two of these tame monsters were imported from South Africa eighteen years ago and gave rise to the rest. This was an attempt to re-establish this splendid species, which was essentially extinct throughout much of its former range due to horn-hungry poachers.

As the sun sank, a herd of 30 large tusked elephants browsed their way across the dry grassland towards the stream in the valley. Mask-faced oryx antelope with long straight horns, reticulated giraffe, zebra, and gazelles peacefully carried on their lives as we watched. Among the thorn bushes stood the solid stoic baobab tree; in the wetter valleys and marshes were fan leaved palms. As we arrived at our camp, a spiral-horned, striped-bodied, lesser kudu calmly crossed the clearing with a group of Thompson's gazelles.

Darkness descended, and Scorpio with Venus at its head hung in the west. In the east the blaze of what I thought was a bush fire gave birth to the fiery full moon.

The baboons and vervet monkeys bedded down in the branches beside our *banda* and barked, grunted, and squealed until finally finding sleep in the safety of the heights.

From Meru, we hit the long dusty road back to Nairobi for showers, sleep, and supplies. The next morning we made the journey back into the middle of Maasai country to Amboseli National Park at the foot of Kilimanjaro. On the parched washboard road, fine powdery dirt filled our truck, and shimmering shapes melted into a mirage as we looked across the bone dry bed of Lake Amboseli and the cloud-covered Kilimanjaro. The thousands of Maasai cattle raised dust to the whipping wind racing across miles of dry semi desert savanna and created a cloud reaching as high as the rain clouds over the mountain. The brightly beaded Maasai wrapped their red blankets tightly against the driving dust.

Amboseli is in the heart of traditional Maasai grazing grounds, and when the park was created in 1972 the Maasai were relocated outside the boundaries, and water was pumped from the marshes out to them and their cattle. This worked well for a few good years and their herds tripled in size. But when there was no fuel to fire the pumps that provide the water, the herds were back in the park marshes and waterholes, displacing the wild animals. The Maasai aren't poachers and only kill wild animals in their various coming-of-age initiation ceremonies and have lived in balance for centuries. A few short years of technological dependence had begun to break the balance.

We set up camp in the palms at the edge of a dry marsh; the palm leaves provided protection from the perpetual dust laden wind. Before sunset the clouds cleared, and we saw the snows of Kilimanjaro. After dark a pair of lions roared on the distant plains. We settled into our lightweight nylon tent, a nebulous shelter from the herd of elephants that tromped, chomped, and trumpeted in the palms within 15 feet of us. I was up several times during the night to keep them from tripping on our tent stakes. Near dawn a lion's roar shook our shelter, and we watched through the mosquito net door as he sauntered by.

The next morning we were treated to the classic pose of a tightly bunched group of white-tusked elephants with the sun-sparkled snows of Kilimanjaro for a backdrop. That afternoon we saw a group of four black rhinos in the tall grass of the marsh with 40 elephants browsing around.

While leaving the park, we witnessed a wildebeest being brought down by a pair of lions and the breath of one being flowing into another. The tourist vans converged faster than the vultures, and I believe were more bloodthirsty, as they crammed for photos of the spectacle. Here I believe tourist development had gone too far in a too exploitative way. The animals were being disturbed and disrespected, and little awareness was gained by tourists of the ways of life as they compete for the best photo.

From Nairobi we took the night train to Mombasa and had an English breakfast served on silver in the polished, wood-paneled dining car. We caught the bus to Malindi along the coast and through the spiny sisal plantations, studded with bare-branched baobabs. The bus got crowded, and African jack-in-the-box music crackled, and the driver's assistant danced in the doorway, ushering in more passengers. We changed buses in Malindi and continued across the Tana River marshes full of birds, baboons, and waterbuck. Kids herded cattle into the fresh water, their villages of domed grass houses not far. Finally the bus stopped at Oceanside and we boarded a dhow to the Arab island of Lamu. A dhow is the age-old, single-mast ship used by Arab slave and spice traders of times past. Now they are used to transport poles from the mangrove swamps to the island for building material. Our first view of the island was of palm-lined beaches, white sand dunes and jade seas–your basic island paradise.

In the village of Lamu the narrow streets, actually alleys, ran between the white washed square stone buildings. The men wore *kikoys*, brightly colored Somalian skirts wrapped around their waists. The island's one car traveled the 200 feet of navigable road daily to the police station. We ate yogurt and fresh fruit at the open-air New Star restaurant and walked the empty beaches.

We returned to Malindi and went snorkeling on the colorful coral reefs with fantastic fish. Tiny brilliant blue fish nestled into the radiantly red coral as huge turtles silently glided by.

Kenya–a land of life and beauty, extending from the coral seas to the desert dryness, the snowy peaks to the flowing plains, where Maasai warriors merge the red in their robes with the blood, the sunset, and the soil of a land alive.

2015

I traveled to Kenya countless times with WWF. What has changed most in Nairobi is the traffic. African cities, built as sleepy colonial posts, now handle hundreds of thousands of vehicles, mostly diesel, snaking slowly across the city. A commute from the airport to town can take hours, as well as just commuting from the office to home.

NINETEEN

The Last Straw

W hat follows is a keynote address I gave during my last year at WWF at a conservation event in Washington, D.C., hosted by Governor Bill Richardson of New Mexico.

You all know the stats, you've seen the press releases regarding ivory seizures on a massive scale and stories of poached elephants every day.

With tiger bone, rhino horn, and elephant ivory now worth more than their weight in gold–one rhino horn alone now has the street value of about $450,000–the trade in animal parts has eclipsed blood diamonds as a source of conflict, especially in Africa, where wildlife crime has become a major source of funding for insurgencies and rebel movements.

Ninety-six elephants were killed each day during 2012. Four elephants per hour, one elephant every 15 minutes. 30,000 this year. Over 62 percent of forest elephants have been killed this decade. Over 700 rhinos killed this year in South Africa: two rhinos a day. Rhino poaching has increased 3,000 percent between the years 2007 and 2011. Three hundred elephants were poisoned with cyanide in Zimbabwe.

More large-scale elephant ivory seizures took place in 2011 than in any other year in the last two decades. A record 24 tons of illegal ivory was seized by customs officials, a ten-fold increase over the previous year.

Globally, the estimated value of the illegal wildlife trade is between $8 and $10 billion a year, more than twice the estimated value of the illegal commerce in small arms, diamonds, gemstones and gold combined.

Adding illegal fishing and timber trades, the wildlife trade would be the fourth largest transnational crime in the world, just behind drugs, counterfeiting, and human trafficking.

The numbers are staggering, representing a true ecological disaster. Seeing it in black and white is startling, but seeing poached elephants on the ground with their tusks hacked out with an ax makes one become a vigilante.

I worked in northern CAR in the late 70's (showing my age). Sudanese horsemen made their annual dry-season trek south across the Bahr Aouk into CAR with huge herds of cattle, setting fires ahead to stimulate a green flush of grass.

The herds were left with herd boys while the horsemen went off carrying huge spears, running down and gutting elephants. With spears alone, they killed 10 percent of the herd in one dry season.

These horsemen became the Janjaweed, terrorizing Darfur, and the spears were replaced by automatic weapons. Herds fell; 85 percent of the elephants died in the hot savanna sun. During the same early 80's, the western black rhino went extinct.

The Janjaweed now have to travel far to find killing fields. They freely cross borders, destabilizing communities and countries. They killed 400 plus elephants in northern Cameroon in 2012, and many more in Chad's Zakouma National Park.

The Lord's Resistance Army (LRA), hiding in these areas between northern DRC and CAR, support their terrorism with ivory.

Al Shabaab, the Somali group believed to be behind the recent mall massacre in Nairobi, fuels its fight with ivory. According to Defense Secretaries Panetta and Hagel in the New York *Times*, Al Shabaab receives up to half its operating funds from ivory sales.

In the Democratic Republic of the Congo (DRC, ex-Zaire), trend data show only a handful of remnant populations of elephants that number more than 500 individuals, with an overall population of no more than 20,000 and declining rapidly, down from an estimated 100,000 as recently as 50 years ago.

In DRC, both the military and militias are implicated in this slaughter, with arms and ammunitions readily available. In Kinshasa, carved ivory still can be bought for $300 per kilogram.

Elephant poaching is organized crime and terrorism. The Vietnamese mafia controls the rhino trade. In Vietnam, there is the mistaken idea that rhino horn has medicinal properties and can even cure cancer.

The demand for ivory is driven by China, the increased middle class and the increased investment and Chinese in Africa. Over one million Chinese businesspeople and workers now live in Africa. China is the major market for ivory.

The trade is being carried out by organized smuggling gangs. Most ivory from Central Africa is shipped via ports in Kenya or Tanzania. Containers filled with hidden ivory are sent on a wild goose chase to foil detection, place of origin, and destination. Although we hear of a lot of seizures, I imagine that less than one in 100 shipments gets caught.

But Africa is a big place. While forest elephants in central Africa have been reduced by over 62 percent in this decade, the majority of elephants occur in stable and growing populations in Southern Africa. Botswana has around 150,000 elephants, with limited poaching. Namibia has well-managed wildlife populations.

Poaching is devastating local populations in parts of the elephant's range, largely Central Africa. In some areas surveyed, the dead elephants outnumber the living elephants.

The demand-mostly Asia, China, Taiwan, Vietnam.

Can the demand be stopped?

Almost two million signatures on a petition delivered to the prime minister of Thailand at the Convention on the International Trade in Endangered Species Conference of Parties (CITES COP) got a commitment to ban ivory exports from that country.

In China the recent success of the WildAid campaign against shark fin has reduced consumption by 50 to 70 percent. Perhaps there is a chance for ivory. Chinese celebrities, like Yao Ming, a basketball star, are urging people not to buy products from endangered species, saying, "When the buying stops, the killing will too."

Can we stop the killing? After the massacre in the north, Cameroon deployed 600 elite troops permanently stationed to protect the northern parks, keeping the poachers at bay.

Gabon and Kenya deployed hundreds of new rangers to protect the wildlife.

In the Dzanga-Sangha Protected Areas network in CAR, good management and dedicated rangers prevented elephant and gorilla poaching for three years. It can be done. The rangers are the real heroes of the fight to stop the killing, and hundreds of them have been killed in the line of duty. I spent 15 years creating and developing Dzanga-Sangha and have witnessed the dedication of rangers protecting their natural heritage.

The same horsemen, responsible for the raid in Northern Cameroon, twice tried to enter Dzanga-Sangha, and were repelled. Only after the Seleka coup, and ensuing chaos, was there a poaching incident in this protected area, in which 26 elephants were killed, likely by these same Sudanese, now associated with the rebel faction, Seleka. We soon mobilized the new government at the central level and have gotten good support from the Seleka that remained to help protect the park, and no further incidents have occurred.

The fact that no single elephant was killed in Dzanga-Sangha from 2010 until the coup is a testament to the success of many years of investment in protected-area management and effective law enforcement.

Dzanga-Sangha is the core of the Sangha Trinational Landscape, designated as a UNESCO World Heritage Site, composed of the contiguous protected areas in Cameroon, CAR, and Congo. There is a trinational brigade which is an anti-poaching force under unified command which is tasked with protecting this large landscape, in recognition that neither elephants nor poachers carry passports or recognize national boundaries. This brigade is bearing good results. One anti-poaching operation in southeast Cameroon netted 90 poaching suspects, of which 52 were tried and convicted.

Through the support of United States Agency for International Development (USAID) and the United States Fish and Wildlife Service (USFWS), we have created 11 similar conservation landscapes in the Congo Basin, from the Mountains of the Moon to the Gulf of Guinea, covering close to 40 percent of the Congo Basin forests.

We are implementing a similar approach in the Ruvuma landscape, spanning the border of Tanzania and Mozambique, and are supporting the largest trans-frontier conservation area in the world, the 440,000 square kilometer Kavongo-Zambizi (KAZA), spanning Botswana, Namibia, Zambia, Zimbabwe, and Angola.

The goal of this huge landscape is to re-create corridors to allow the elephants the freedom to roam, expanding from overly concentrated populations in Botswana to areas emptied by conflict in Angola. The governments of these five countries have signed a treaty to create KAZA to break down the barriers between countries so that elephants can expand their range instead of being culled and tourists can circulate through the many parks with one visa for KAZA. WWF is extending its successful Community Based Natural Resource Management Program (CBNRM) in Namibia into KAZA.

In Namibia, 79 conservancies have provided the communities the means to manage local lands and wildlife. The conservancies engage more than one in eight Namibians in conservation, who now manage some 30 million acres, more than 15 percent of the country. By extending this program through KAZA, the local people will benefit and thrive on their natural heritage.

Wise sustainable-use programs have resulted in very little poaching on Namibia's conservancies, as the people own their wildlife resources. Over 45 percent of Namibia is designated for wildlife management. Namibia has the largest free-ranging population of black rhinos in Africa.

In a more general sense, an overall failure of conservation and enforcement in Africa has been within the judiciary sector. Too often poachers are released without charges as a result of corruption or incompetence. We have identified an urgent need to strengthen the rule of law at all levels, from evidence collection at the scene of the crime all the way through to conviction and sentencing, with media coverage and public awareness playing a key role in shining daylight on these cases to minimize the likelihood of corruption.

We feel that it is time to recognize that rule of law extends to protected areas and anti-poaching, and without it, no country can be considered to have adequate governance. Governance begins at the site level.

Wildlife crime is too often treated as a petty crime or a nuisance rather than a serious crime on par with extortion, money laundering, tax evasion or trafficking of other illicit items. In reality, it is often linked with all of these serious crimes. Wildlife crime is low risk/high gain—we are trying to change this equation.

As we have seen with the well-armed Sudanese Janjaweed-type militias in Central Africa, poaching of elephants for ivory is also an issue of sovereignty and national security, with criminal elements linked to insurgency and warfare.

The poaching crisis has reached the highest political levels. President Obama pledged $10 million to help stop the killing. The Clinton Global Initiative has pledged $80 million to stop the killing, trade, and demand and to double the ranger force in key areas of Africa.

Heads of state (HOS) from African countries are taking stands, making wildlife crime a serious crime, increasing penalties, and urging Asian countries to halt imports. The COMIFAC (Commission of Forest of Central Africa) has adopted a regional anti-poaching pact, pledging zero tolerance for poaching and increased penalties for wildlife crimes, and eliminating the internal and external ivory trade. The Economic Community of Central Africa is dedicating part of the upcoming HOS summit in Paris to combating wildlife crime in the region.

President Bongo of Gabon shared the stage with the Clintons this year (2015), and at the last 2 U.N. General Assemblies, he has made pledges committing his country to treat wildlife crime as a serious offense, reinforcing protection and the judiciary, and urging other countries to do the same.

Two years ago, President Bongo burned the entire Gabonese stock of ivory to show the world and his country that poaching will no longer be tolerated. Now that our own government is back in business, our ivory crush has been rescheduled (and since occurred). We need leaders, and they are emerging. Now we need real action to stop the illegal slaughter.

WWF has always worked to protect flagship species. This year, however they've redoubled their efforts and launched a global Illegal Wildlife Crimes campaign, focusing on rhinos, elephants, and tigers. We want to change the equation from low risk, high gain to the opposite. You may have seen WWF's posters around town.

Tigers are not coats.
Rhinos are not medicine.
Elephants are not trinkets.

WWF wants to leave our children a living planet. We need to work together to continue to foster solid field conservation efforts, improved technologies for law enforcement, and provide an improved livelihood for local people. We will continue to work from Pygmy paths to parliament halls to keep life in business. We need to stop the killing. Stop the trafficking. Stop the demand. And we need to support sound, sustainable management.

In Conclusion

The Ivory trade, once an obscure issue, is now in every American's living room. The power of the concerted campaign has raised awareness tremendously. As I write this in September 2015, the copy of *National Geographic,* with its feature story on ivory, sits on my desk. The numbers keep increasing, of poached elephants, pangolins, etc., and the price tags are up to $19 billion a year for the illegal wildlife trade. Almost every head of state in Africa has made lofty statements, quoting the same figures and issuing harsh warnings of impending crackdowns on poaching in their territory, certainly to stop the foreign terrorists and mafias, certainly on the increase, that they are suddenly aware of.

But beware the lofty statements. Few countries are actually putting more boots on the ground to effectively fight this battle. Gabon is one, Botswana and Namibia, others. The greatest obstacles are the lack of real obstacles to poachers. "Compromised governance" has created the enabling conditions of corruption and compliance. Why is Africa behind in development, when air-conditioned SUVs full of foreign experts clog the streets of every African capital? The development business has built lots of villas, I've even heard of the Ebola business in West Africa, built from the billions of foreign aid. Corruption and graft are human conditions that exist everywhere but reached a high art form in much of Africa.

"Never say never" is a strategy for the Peter Pan politicians in parts of Africa. In Cameroon, for example, there is not one protected area that doesn't have at least two, if not more, conflicting land uses. I've seen maps and field realities of mining and logging leases within parks and other protected areas. Even World Heritage Sites (WHS) are within this never-neverland. I mentioned earlier that the five WHS in DRC are all declared as "In Danger." Rebel groups and warring factions have used these isolated forest areas as hideouts, raping and pillaging villages, living on wildlife, and buying arms with ivory profits. Virunga, Africa's first National Park (Albert NP) and the home to the endangered mountain gorillas, is a case in point. During the Rwanda genocide, refugee camps hosting millions of displaced people in and along the Virunga, with the only wood for cooking coming from the park, devastated the forests. Many rebel groups, from the Mai-Mai to the M-23, used these mountain forests as refuge.

On another front, the Virunga witnessed another fight for its existence. A United Kingdom-based oil company, SOCO, was granted permission to "explore" for oil within the park boundary. This set off an international outcry, as UNESCO (which administers the WH program), WWF, and many others appealed to the DRC government to respect their own laws and the international WH Convention, which does not permit oil exploitation within a World Heritage Site. This prolonged controversy is depicted in the movie *Virunga*, and pits Prince Emmanuel de Merode, Virunga park manager, against the shady SOCO scouts and rebel soldiers. So far, the government of DRC has upheld the law, and de Merode survived an assassination attempt. This is the classic case of conservation in a conflict zone.

A less dramatic situation occurred in the Selous Game Reserve, in Tanzania. Entrepreneurs and the Tanzanian government decided it was time to exploit a major uranium deposit on the southern side of Selous. The UNESCO decision to modify the boundary of Selous came as hard rock mining, oil, and gas have become major threats to protected areas throughout Africa, from Mozambique to Murchison Falls, Uganda.

Minerals have fueled many conflicts. Conflict and chaos allow militias control of mineral-rich areas. Coltan (colombo-tantalite) was known as "blood tantalite" by some trying to embargo the mineral from the war zones of DRC. In the early 2000's, everyone had a cell phone, and millions of play stations and the like were sold around the world. Coltan is used in these devices to regulate voltage and store energy, so we all are complicit in this conflict. Kahuzi-Biega National Park, also a WHS in Eastern DRC, was the center of the coltan finds. Kahuzi-Biega is home to the eastern lowland gorilla, like the mountain gorilla, a sub-species of the eastern gorilla. Conservation groups walked a fine line as coltan mining became one of the only ways for displaced Congolese farmers to eke out a living in this war torn land. Much of Kahuzi-Biega, a long time hideout for the Mai-Mai, is now overrun with miners and farmers.

Conservation Organizations, including WWF, have made great achievements, saving species and habitats hand in hand with local communities and dedicated host-government partners. Notable examples mentioned are the Namibia CBNRM program, Dzanga-Sangha, and the park system in Gabon. Programs promoting local ownership in which investment reaches the people most concerned about wildlife, the communities and indigenous peoples whose lives depend on natural resources, have been somewhat successful.

But big conservation, like a big ship, is slow to steer. On the one hand, it provides a steady course, and the successes cited are those that have benefited from long-term investment and persistence. With a big ship, minor course corrections keep you ahead of the winds of change. Geographic scope, for instance, was a gradual shifting by degrees from a species/site level, from parks to landscapes, from country to regional programs. WWF and others created programs to address major global threats such as the footprint of food, consumption, and climate change. However, about every three years, the five-year plans are turned 90 to 180 degrees, causing major disruptions in programs, people, and results. More and more staff time is spent in planning meetings, planning, re-planning, navel gazing, attending conferences, and workshops amounting to 60 to 80 percent of a country director's time. It's hard to coordinate conservation in Lusaka from a hotel in Lausanne!

However challenging the past and current situation in Africa is, what looms ahead could spell opportunity, or disaster, but certainly great change. Currently, with a few exceptions, such as the fertile volcanic soils of the highlands of eastern DRC and Rwanda, Africa's population density is relatively low. It's a big continent, with sparse population. As Max Fisher reported in the *Washington Post* in July 2013, that's changing very quickly–Africa's population is expected to expand by 400 percent in just 90 years. That's four times the workforce, four times the resource burden, four times the voters that will transform political and social dynamics within Africa and African countries' relationships with the rest of the world. Africa will have almost as many people as Asia by 2100, growing by a factor of 5.18, and this rapid growth will bring fundamental changes. The African Century, or African curse? Two factors crucial for Asian success, good governance and careful resource management, are not well known in most of Africa. Exploding population growth may well worsen resource competition–food, water, electricity–making political instability and conflict even more likely. There will be a "youth bulge" making instability inevitable unless jobs can be created.

Life spans in the African Century are expected to rise by 50 percent, and the birth rate is 4.9 children per woman, hard to slow down for cultural and economic reasons, but leading to a youth bulge needing food, jobs, and livelihoods. Only 56 percent of Africans are of working age, with a huge dependent cohort of the very young, which partially explains the proliferation of child soldiers.

Nigeria alone, about the size of Texas, already Africa's most populous country, is expected to increase by a factor of eight in just 100 years–almost a billion people and poised to surpass China in population. Nigeria is the poster child of corruption, poverty, conflict. How will a government respond when the demand on resources, social services, schools, and roads increase eight fold? Oil wealth, which has fueled the above-mentioned ills of corruption and conflict, will not likely prepare them for this future.

Tanzania, one of the world's poorest countries, grew from 34 million in 2000 to 45 million today, and an expected whopping 276 million, almost the same as the U.S., by 2100; Ethiopia and DRC are projected to be as large.

This rapid population growth comes as the climate dries and water and resources become scarcer. We are faced with the nexus of population explosion, climate change, resource depletion, biodiversity loss. Already crowded cities will grow as people seek jobs. The African Century–how will they/we cope? New, dynamic African leaders, from NEPAD (New Partnership for Africa's Development of the African Union), individual countries, and communities will need to find synergies to balance investment, job creation, efficient agriculture and food production, biodiversity conservation, rural futures and urban planning, all in the context of climate change. It can be done and has begun, and my hope is that a new dynamism will overcome the old inertia and the African Century will be bright.

My *kete kodoro na be ti Afrique*–little home in the heart of Africa–is not off to a good start. The United Nations International Crisis Group for CAR[7] just issued a troubling report this month. Quoting from the Executive Summary, "Crisis in the Central African Republic is long-term and characterized by sporadic surges of violence against a backdrop of state disintegration, a survival economy and deep inter-ethnic cleavages. Armed groups (including the anti-balaka and the ex-Seleka) are fragmenting and becoming increasingly criminalized; intercommunal tensions have hampered efforts to promote CAR's national unity and mend its social fabric." *Zo kwe zo.*

Again, it seems that the illicit mineral quest is driving, or at least thriving, in the chaos and lawlessness. One of the recommendations in the same report cited above is directed to the United Nation MINUSCA forces and the French Sangaris (the title of the French intervention forces in CAR). Recommendation No. 3 states, "Regain control of the main gold and diamond production sites by deploying international forces and CAR civil servants and revive the Kimberly Process certification scheme for diamonds originating from these controlled areas. An investigative unit addressing diamond, gold and ivory trafficking, as well as militarized poaching should also be integrated into MINUSCA." It goes on to recommend that the French delay the departure of their forces "in order to maintain the capacity for military pressure to induce armed groups to disarm." Basically, foreign military must bolster the disintegrated state and provide some modicum of order.

I just got off the phone with my friend Kpanou, Jean Bosco mentioned earlier in happier times. He is back in Dzanga-Sangha doing ecological monitoring. He received panicked calls from his kids in Bangui today–after a few months of relative calm, gun shots again rung in downtown Bangui.

In my early chapters, I compared Bokassa to his neighbor to the south in Zaire (now DRC), Mobutu. The neighboring countries remain on a parallel path of plunder and pathetic "governance." DRC has had a U.N. force of about 20,000 Blue Hats since 1999 and the chaos continues.

So where does this leave the rosy optimism of the 23-year-old after 35 years of this downward spiral in Central Africa. Dzanga-Sangha lives on, elephants thrive in the salty wallows of the Dzanga *bai*, my legacy carried on by dedicated Central Africans and supporters who have seen over the years that maintaining a disciplined field force can keep pace with the poaching pressure. However, there has been a steady decline in smaller animals, such as duikers, the small antelope that the BaAka depend on for food. There has been a parallel decline in the health and nutrition status of the BaAka, who are now supplementing more and more through agriculture. Against all odds, it is still among the richest forests in Central Africa.

And Manovo-Gounda Saint Floris? Cattle are doing quite well, wild-life is all but gone. I mentioned the book *La Chasses Oubliée*-the forgotten hunt. For me, the memories will remain, but the lifeblood of the heart of Africa will be forgotten, never known, by the new generations trying to find their way in the African Century.

As for myself, "retired" from WWF and retreated from Africa. I had the advantage of longevity, persistence that permitted me to see the spiral of repeated history. I was able to anticipate problems, as they are simply recycled. Now I've turned my attention to my own backyard. I serve on the boards of three dynamic North Carolinian organizations. Discover Life in America, having completed a 15-year, All Taxa Biodiversity Inventory (ATBI) in the Great Smoky Mountains National Park, discovering 8,000 new species for the park and 1,000 new species for science, has turned its attention to fostering a Global Biodiversity Census. I recently joined the board of the North Carolina Zoological Society, to help strengthen the conservation component. I help the Triangle Land Conservancy on its Conservation Committee, developing land stewardship in the Raleigh-Durham region of North Carolina.

And actually in my own backyard, I have transformed a chickweed-filled lawn to 2,000 square feet of raised beds, and I've become a suburban farm-er. I call it my victory garden and my bit to reduce the footprint of food pro-duction. During the Second World War, when the term victory garden was coined, over 40 percent of the food produced and consumed in the U.S. was from backyard farms. So, smarter people will help sort out Africa, while I hoe beans in my backyard.

ACKNOWLEDGEMENTS

It was a simple twist of fate, as Dylan sang, perhaps, that took me from the mountains and my marine biology path to Central Africa. I am forever indebted to the United States Peace Corps for providing me with the infrastructure to have these life experiences. And I thank Peace Corps Writers for publishing this little story. I was posted in CAR for five years with Peace Corps, although I remained in CAR for another decade. The knowledge of the country and language gained in my Peace Corps years gave me a foundation to carry on. For that decade, and 20 more years, the World Wildlife Fund provided that vehicle to carry out my life's mission. My career with WWF was "right livelihood," using whatever talent I had to foster life on earth. WWF remains mission-driven and is trying its best to leave our children a living planet.

Tony Mokombo, a friend now for 40 years, was my first friend in Central Africa. His kind, calm demeanor helped me adapt in a different world. Tony eventually came to Washington as WWF's program officer for Central Africa. He still lives in Maryland where he as serves as a pastor. Kpanou, Jean Bosco, started with me as a shy young man in Boganangone, feeding fish and planting gardens. I said to Jean that if he was always straight with me, didn't lie, I would help him develop. He went with me to the forests of Dzanga-Sangha, was my right-hand friend doing soup-to-nuts work to develop this incredible protected-area system, and he won the prestigious Goldman Award for conservation achievement. François, Baba George, Thimotée, Jean Fio, and all the "fish agents," were friends, ambassadors for, and the backbone of, the fisheries program. Zongoina, Clements, helped me fit into fireside chats in Boganangone and be part of the community. Phillip Hunsicker, dubbed Pig Pen as his Peace Corps nickname, lived 60 k's south of me in Boda, and was my closest Peace Corps friend. We drank many a warm Mocaf and *Kongoya* with the fish agents and with good humor got a lot of good work done. Phil eventually joined me in Dzanga-Sangha as a rural development specialist, fostering sustainable development in this Integrated Conservation and Development Program.

Bruce Hurlberg, my partner in MGSF, played the accordion and danced Norwegian folk dances. He said "poop;" I was more explicit. He wore khaki, I wore as little as possible. We'd be 50 kilometers away from base camp, hiking through amazing wilderness, and he would ask me what I wanted for dinner when we reached camp–the last thing on my mind. We were polar opposites, and we were the best of friends. The Ecoguard in Manovo-Gounda Saint Floris, huge Zotara, slit the throat of a zebu bull illegally grazing in the park, while wearing a `World Peace through Vegetarianism" T-shirt I had given him. Etienne, lean and hard, *sec* (dry) could walk a hundred miles without a drop of water. And Luc, murdered by poachers on the border with Sudan with his feet and hands removed–these are the heroes of MGSF that I will never forget.

Monsieur Cabaille, the Honorary Inspector of Hunting, was the first hunting inspector in Ubangui-Shari as part of the colonial regime. I knew him at age 80 or so in MGSF. His two gold-capped canine teeth reflected the sun as he laughed. We would go for drives in his Land Rover, and precisely at noon, no matter where we were, he'd stop, unlash the table and chairs, unfold the table cloth, and break out pâté and baguettes. When he had a hunting camp in Northern CAR, all the hunting guides would congregate to his camp on Sundays. He would ceremoniously measure the precise amount of cinnamon stick, nutmeg, and other secret ingredients of his famous rum punch. Eliza Spessard saved my life on the Ouaka River, was my advocate in Bangui, and is a lifelong friend.

The *Cheshire Herald*, the local paper from Cheshire Connecticut, published many of these chapters as periodic articles, translated from chicken scratch by my sister Lynn. Nancy Kittle, friend and supporter of WWF, typed the first Word document of this book. My wonderful wife, Doreen Collins, made some sense of my prose through prudent editing. Jennifer Koontz–still able to sing the Sango rap songs she learned when she visited me in CAR in the 90s–did the detailed copy editing that was so needed.

Most of all, I write this for my children, Deva, Orion, and Dylan, that these stories often heard, may be remembered.

REFERENCES

1. *The Congo: Plunder & Resistance.* David Renton, David Seddon, and Leo Zeilig. London and New York: Zed Books, 2007.

2. *Lord Leverhulme's Ghosts: Colonial Exploitation in the Congo.* Jules Marchal. London and New York: Verso. 2009.

3. *Great Britain and the Congo: The Pillage of the Congo Basin.* Edmund Dene Morel. BiblioLife 2009.

4. *King Leopold's Ghost: A Story of Greed, Terror, and Heroism in Colonial Africa.* Adam Hochschild. Mariner Books. 1998.

5. *La Chasse Oubliée.* Jean-Luc Temporal. Gerfaut Club. 1989.

6. *The amazing, surprising, Africa-driven demographic future of the Earth, in 9 charts.* The Washington Post. Max Fisher. July, 2013.

7. United Nations International Crisis Group for CAR. Report and Recommendations. 2015.

www.ingramcontent.com/pod-product-compliance
Lightning Source LLC
Chambersburg PA
CBHW051831090426
42736CB00011B/1756